Pure Pleasures

Luscious Live Food Recipes from the Glowing Temple Kitchen

by Natalia

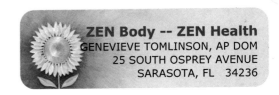

S0-AIJ-366

glowing temple

www.glowingtemple.com

First Edition

Food Styling and Photography by Natalia www.glowingtemple.com
Cover and Book Design by Adam Mills / Bottomless Design www.bottomlessdesign.com
Cover Photo, Back Cover Photo and photos on pages 107, 117, 127 by Jerah Coviello www.ecovogue365.com
Edited by Justin Karoway-Waterhouse

ISBN-10: 1453797866
ISBN-13: 9781453797860

All of the information contained in this book is based on my personal experience. This book is not to be treated as or to take the place of medical advice from a qualified health care professional. In the case of serious illness, please seek professional assistance.

To my lovelove Adam—my favorite person to feed.

Also to family and friends—the meals we have shared
are my true source of inspiration.

 XOXO

CONTENTS

A Love Letter from Natalia

I am a girl with a burning passion for a pleasure-filled lifestyle and I need to share it with you. I have learned over the years that the things I stick with are the ones that make me feel ecstatic. We all keep going back to certain things time after time, because, well, it feels really good. This is what Pure Pleasures is all about: indulging in delicious pure foods, loving the way you look and feel, and then going back for more.

Let me back up a bit. Lots of people look to live food for weight loss, healing and cleansing. That is what brought me here. I originally turned to live food for healing. I had been battling with Candida for years. For a young woman, barely over 20, I had taken far too many antibiotics for my little body to handle. My body was completely imbalanced and overrun with yeast and bacteria. I had spent several years under treatment from handfuls of practitioners, all to no avail. There were restrictive diets and massive amounts of supplements, not to mention the thousands of dollars I spent. No matter what I did, I noticed no improvement. None. What I did notice was a recurring theme of deprivation, diet, discipline and hard work. None of what I was doing was joyful. So, I quit. One day I decided that I was going to heal from within. I did not know how and I did not know when, but I was going to do it. I remember calling my brother Justin for advice when I came to this realization. How fortunate for me that he had been studying live foods, in school no less. He shared what he knew about cleansing and boosting my immune system. Most importantly, he finished with a concept that was entirely new to me—a total WAKE UP CALL. As much as I could work on healing my body, it was just as important to look at the emotional factors involved. HELLOOOOO!!! This was revolutionary to me. I knew that negative thoughts were not conducive to healing, but this was the first time that I had heard that the lack of pleasure in my life could have specifically been encouraging my illness. I immediately turned to live foods to heal physically and also found a holistic counselor to work with on emotional healing. At that point, things finally began to change.

Wow. So, you know what I did next? I did things that I always wanted to do. I quit my job (oh that felt good). I moved to Florida where the sun is always shining bright (this is getting better). I connected with people who really got me (now this is getting addictive). I traveled to amazing, life altering, exotic destinations (ohhh, the pleasure). I started my own business (can it get any better than this?). I met even more amazing people (yes it can). I created a new theme for my life and it is one of pleasure. Through it all, one truth has remained constant—I feel amazing when I treat my body like a temple. Enjoying pure foods is a full circle of pleasure that I want you to experience. It has to begin from the moment you shop. Enjoy going out and finding the freshest, cleanest produce available. Bring it all home and play in your kitchen, experimenting with exotic spices, fine oils, raw nuts and seeds. Now have a seat and deeply enjoy the pleasure of every indulgent taste. It gets even better. Feel how nourished you are. Watch your body cleanse what is no longer needed. Feel how light and energized you become. Notice just how much pleasure you have created for yourself and then reach for more.

I am creating because I am passionate about pure food, sharing because I believe in my lifestyle and indulging because I can, want to, and it makes me happy. My lesson has been in allowing myself these joys and to let go of the things I feel like I have to do. In the long run, the habits you keep are those in which you find the most pleasure; not fleeting pleasure, but full circle pleasure. Try these recipes, enjoy the preparation, indulge in the flavors, and follow the bliss that is coming your way. What I share has been my unique experience. I only wish to inspire you to discover your path to pleasure.

With love and wishes of bliss!

Natalia

MY LIVE FOOD LIFESTYLE

The Raw and Living food movement is growing. At this point you have probably heard about it: read a blurb in a magazine, caught a glimpse of it on some hip television show, or found out some celebrity is supporting it. I have been there. The idea had been hinted at me for years, more in that fashionable sort of way. I remember picking up a live food recipe book in 2003 at an Urban Outfitters in Providence, RI. It was gorgeous, hip, fresh and was being sold alongside the latest fashions. It had a sort of trend-factor.

Chances are, you already eat raw food. You might have fruit for breakfast, eat salads or snack on raw nuts. Your whole life you have heard that fresh food is good for you. That is impossible to ignore. So you are already enjoying raw foods, great news!

When you break it down into simple terms, this is real food. Food that is fresh, organic and alive! It has never been cooked, treated or processed. Everything is made from fruits, vegetables, nuts, seeds and sprouts in all of their delicious and creative forms. Raw foods are just that; raw and uncooked. Living foods are those that have been sprouted and germinated. Soaked nuts, sprouted seeds and grains are full of live enzymes. Combining these two basic groups sounds simple, and it is, but wait until you see where this can take you. These fresh, whole foods contain maximum life force, vitamins, minerals and active enzyme content contributing to your overall health and well-being. You know you want to feel this good.

My approach to raw and living foods is not that of a diet. This is my lifestyle. You choose how much you want to incorporate into your life. Your mind, body and spirit will let you know what is perfect for you. I have found that it is hard to stay joyful while looking at this as some sort of restrictive diet. For me, it has to be about what I can eat, how many gourmet combinations of these foods I can impress myself with and what I am indulging in. Looking at things with this perspective opened me up to meet new people, try new activities, reach new heights of success in my professional life and to become truly happy and fulfilled. What began as a change in my food choices is now a change in my entire being. The more raw, organic and living food you can incorporate into your day, the more that I see these possibilities opening up for you. This has been my experience, what I have seen through my own life and those I surround myself with. I talk with friends of the magic that the lifestyle brings to me on a daily basis and really, I could discuss it to no end. But I am one of those people who will believe anything, as long as I have experienced it. You have to experience the magic for yourself. You know you want to. Be open and let it in.

TOP 10 LIVE FOOD KITCHEN TIPS

1. **Give your kitchen a little makeover!** You don't need everything right away, but you are going to want to make sure you have a few essential tools to begin: sharp knives, a peeler, big bowls, a cutting board and when you're ready…
   - FOOD PROCESSOR Any basic model with an S-blade and a shredding disc will do.
   - HIGH SPEED BLENDER Get the best blender for your budget. You are going to want something powerful that will really turn hard nuts into smooth creams.
   - DEHYDRATOR Though not a complete necessity, dehydrators offer us a way to create different textures for breads, crackers, snacks and wraps that are so pleasurable. I have given dehydration times in ranges as they may vary depending on the humidity of your climate.
   - MANDOLINE Pull this out when you want a really thin and uniform slice.
   - MICROPLANE This is great for zesting citrus and grating fresh ginger.
   - CITRUS JUICER Whether it is a hand held reamer or an electric juicer, you are going to want something to help you juice lots of citrus fast.
   - JUICER Green veggie juices are a feel-good staple! Find a juicer that fits your budget and get juicy.

② Understand soaking and sprouting. In living foods, we soak nuts and seeds to remove their enzyme inhibitors—compounds inherent in nature to prevent premature sprouting. Through soaking, we activate sprouting capabilities, boost the nutritional benefit and allow for ease of digestion. You can take this a step further with some seeds to the point of actually growing green sprouts. For all purposes in this book, we are only aiming for activation. You will notice with each recipe, there are different soaking instructions based on the type of nut or seed. With Brazil nuts, we will skip the soaking process as they do not contain enzyme inhibitors. You will often see me using Brazil nuts for dessert crusts or to substitute walnuts when I haven't had the time to plan ahead for soaking. Some nuts and seeds will be used directly after soaking and others will need to be dehydrated until they are crisp again.

③ Go organic! I cannot overstress the importance of true organic foods. To me, it is not so much what is on a label, but more about knowing my farmer and the growing methods used. It is so important to support organic farmers. It is better for your health, it is better for the health of the farmers and better for our earth. Get committed and do the best you can in the part of the world that you live in. If you can grow your own, even better!

④ Be prepared. Raw food preparation can be a little different from your average cooking. My best advice is to set aside a few blocks of time each week to stock up on your favorite staples. I will cut veggies, wash greens, and make dressings in bulk so that I always have a nourishing salad ready in minutes. I make pâtés, dips and dehydrated breads to keep on hand for quick lunches and dinners. I keep bananas frozen for quick, frosty smoothies. Oh, and of course desserts—I usually make one sweet each week, store it in the freezer and take a piece out, one by one. It may seem daunting to spend a few hours in the kitchen at a time, but this is the key to success, making sure that when you are hungry, there is always something to grab.

⑤ Superfoodies! There are lots of fun ingredients that I have discovered through live foods. The recipes in this book may be a first introduction for some of you. Below are a few ingredients that you will meet in the following pages. You can be sure to find these using my resources at the back of this book.

- Cacao is simply raw chocolate. I use it in powder, nib and butter form. The powder is great for smooth chocolate desserts. The nibs can be used like a quick chocolate chip replacement. You'll get to know the butter as a liquid fat to make some amazing cake icings. The butter will most likely be solid when you buy it, but it melts at just over 90° F, either in your dehydrator or warmed double boiler.
- Chia Seed is an ancient Aztec staple. It makes an amazing tapioca-like pudding and holds dehydrated goods together in the same sticky way that flax seed does.
- Coconut Aminos is my favorite soy sauce alternative—like a soy-free soy sauce! Say what? This is made from fermented coconut sap and is perfect in all of your favorite Asian inspired recipes. If it is not readily available to you, feel free to substitute Nama Shoyu, wheat-free tamari, or soy aminos.
- Coconut Butter is a creamy spread made from a combination of the oil and meat of coconuts. It is lightly sweet, super rich and complements many desserts.
- Coconut Flour is the must have ingredient for my very special cake recipes. This flour is the remaining, dehydrated fiber after the oil has been removed from a coconut.
- Coconut Oil is a rich, major health boosting oil that I love for desserts. It is a liquid at 76° F and above and solid below. For all recipes, if solid, melt in your dehydrator, in the sun, or in a warmed double boiler.
- Hemp Seed is such a staple for me! You will see how often this gets used in my recipes. It tastes great, blends up creamy and makes a lovely garnish when sprinkled on top of food.
- Himalayan Crystal Salt, unlike common table salt, is full of minerals and health benefits. Make the switch today!
- Kombucha is a cultured tea full of essential probiotics, enzymes, amino acids and anti-oxidants. It has been consumed throughout the world for hundreds of years to promote health and longevity.
- Lucuma is a luscious Peruvian fruit that is dried for our use as a low sugar sweetener with a subtle maple flavor. It is so yummy with chocolate and in creamy smoothies.
- Purple Corn Kernels are another Peruvian wonder. This heirloom corn is full of antioxidants and phytonutrients. It is sold dried in the states as it is not commercially grown here. It is the key ingredient in my Purple Corn Chips (*page 47*).

6. **Learn the lingo.** While shopping for food, you are going to want to be armed with knowledge. You want to know that you are getting truly raw, high quality products. You have to do a little research, but you will surely get the hang of it. We are lucky that raw food is gaining popularity and some labels are even using the word "raw" to help us out. Oils, like coconut, olive, sesame and hemp should be cold-pressed. Nuts and seeds should be labeled raw and organic (see tip 7 for more dirt on this topic). Dried fruits should be organic and labeled sun dried or low-temperature dried and of course, sulfur dioxide-free.

7. **Know your source.** When I decided to go raw, it was important for me to know that what I was eating was, in fact, raw. I began to learn different things about what was going on in the food industry that would affect my food choices. For example, many almonds that are labeled "raw" at your health food store are pasteurized (cooked). Almost all raw cashews are heated during the shelling process. Companies that were selling raw cacao admitted that high temperatures were being reached in processing. The same goes for some nut butters. I have found my favorite sources for truly raw nuts (including cashews and almonds), seeds, cacao, oils, butters and more. I have included them in my resources section at the back of the book. They are sourcing ingredients with the utmost integrity. When in doubt, just ask for the facts and trust your instincts. It is not the end of the world if you eat something that is not raw. However, it has always been important for me to make sure this would be a conscious decision rather than a mistake due to a corporation's lack of integrity.

8. **Break the rules!** I love to encourage creativity in the kitchen. It is so much fun to play around and experiment. I offer my recipes as guidelines and inspiration. They totally rock, but feel free to add or subtract according to your taste. I also want you to be comfortable with all of the ingredients. I'm almost vegan, though I do consume bee products. I love raw honey for its amazing nutritional profile. Some vegans I know choose not to consume honey and I completely respect that. I use clear agave, sometimes when I need a certain texture, or to be honest, when I am out of honey. There has been a lot of controversy surrounding agave in the health world lately…is it low glycemic or high glycemic? Is it raw or cooked? This is all hard for me to answer as I have read up on both sides of the story. I choose to trust my suppliers and listen to my body. When used sparingly, I feel just fine with the clear, raw agave. Try it for yourself—experiment with sweeteners and use what gives you the most pleasure.

9. **KISS! Keep it Simple, Silly!** I love to eat very gourmet and I definitely follow my "be prepared" tip. That does not change the fact that my life is super busy and I am always on the go. You will often find me out and about with a green smoothie, an apple or a banana. Things that you can just grab and go are so important. You may also find that your body loves these mono meals of fruits, having only one food to digest at a time. I encourage you to enjoy these simple pleasures.

10. **The more, the merrier.** Whenever possible, make meals with friends and family. It is so much more fun to create together…or in the case of me and my hubby, to get help with the dishes. With your own little team, you can get so much more accomplished in a shorter time.

TOP 10 LIVE FOOD LIFESTYLE TIPS

1. **Relax!** This does not have to be an all or nothing game. Do the absolute best you can. If you make the choice to indulge in something, never allow any feelings of guilt or regret. Accept that it has given you what you needed at that moment, be grateful and move on.

2. **Drink the purest water** you can get your hands on. Can you go out and collect water from a fresh spring? This is the best option possible! Can you juice and get lots of your liquids from pure organic fruits and veggies? Otherwise, again, we do the best we can. Just make sure it is clean—no fluoride, chlorine…basically no straight up tap water. Also, try to avoid traditional bottled water in plastic. Lots of times this is essentially tap water

quality, leaching chemicals from its plastic bottle. Do some research and find out the best purification system for the type of water in your area. Filter it as cleanly as possible and see if you can also find a way to restructure the water through certain systems, crystals, prayer, magnets and more. Find out what speaks to you.

3 **Be proud of what you are doing.** Celebrate the fact that you're taking charge of your well-being. You may meet people along the way that project their discomfort of your uniqueness onto you. Sure, this may not be a mainstream lifestyle today, but you rock for being who you are and doing what you believe in. Though preaching raw foodie dogma is not my style, I love to stand up and say I live this lifestyle because I feel amazing and love my life. If that is ever met with opposition, I know that it is not my issue to deal with.

4 **Inspire.** Share food with friends and family. Though there may always be people in your life that choose to eat another way, it's a beautiful feeling to share a meal of live foods, prepared lovingly, with those who are new to it. I have been toting my own meals to gatherings for years. Happy Thanksgiving everyone, I brought my own lunch! I always bring enough to share and find that everyone feels more comfortable.

5 **Get out and find support.** I am really comfortable with my lifestyle, close to three years in. In the beginning, it was different. There were so many people with questions and opinions of the way I was choosing to eat. It was crucial for me to find people who were doing the same thing. Raw foodies are everywhere now! Where is your local group? Do your best to connect with others, share meals, recipes and support for the amazing things you are all doing. It feels so good.

6 **Listen to your inspiration.** When you really get into this lifestyle, some things may begin to change. You may realize that there are parts of your life that you are ready to let go of. Some may require work and others will just fall away. There will be new things that you are going to want to take on and experience. Be open to what you are seeing and feeling. Take the time to get out into nature and meditate if that speaks to you. Follow your heart and your bliss.

7 **Connect with your body.** Before live food, I was eating at all hours, hungry or not, because I felt like it or thought I had to. Now, my eating habits really flow in a much more natural and healthy way. People are always pushing breakfast. Sure, I want some nutrition in the morning, but when you are breaking your overnight fast (break-fast) you want to be gentle on your body. I will drink lots of water in the morning, sometimes with lemon and some super green powder. I will not eat however, until I feel truly hungry. The same goes for the rest of the day. I eat when I feel hungry and I do my best to stop when I feel satisfied and not full. I also avoid eating late at night for proper digestion. Your body will tell you what works for you and what does not, just be open to understand the difference.

8 **Move it!** This is one thing I have to keep reminding myself. Exercise is that thing that always gets passed over when I am busy. It is seriously one of the most important things you can do for your health. You have got to find something that you love and make it a habit. There are so many options. Dance, practice yoga, run, hula hoop, walk, swim…what inspires you? Take your pick and just get out and do it!

9 **Travel.** There has been no better teacher of who I am and what my purpose is than the traveling I have done. Whether it is between states or running to the complete opposite side of the world, experiencing different cultures is such an illuminating experience. There is no substitute. My absolute favorite traveling experience is to taste exotic fruits for the first time—such a simple pleasure. Pick places that are known for their abundance of fresh foods and you will surely eat well.

10 **Have a total blast!** Throw a chocolate dance party. Host a live food potluck picnic. Serve up a fancy brunch to your friends. When you're living a life of pure pleasure, it's the time to celebrate everything and anything with amazing food and fabulous company.

DRINK IT UP!

As a raw foodie, I get a lot of my nutrition, satisfaction and pleasure from liquids. Juices and smoothies are fast, and when you're busy, they're great for an on-the-go lifestyle. I am always out and about with a glass jar full of something yummy. Green, red, pink, purple...hot colors and cool drinks full of flavor, nutrients and energy. Cheers to pure liquid pleasure!

CHOCOLATE SILK SHAKE

When I speak of pure pleasure, a recipe like this is the essence of my meaning. This is a super thick, luscious shake made with pure, raw ingredients. It's so super yummy, words can hardly do it justice. Blend it up and taste for yourself…now!

Serves 2

INGREDIENTS

½ cup pure water
1 ripe Hass avocado
¾ cup raw cashews, soaked 1 hour, drained/rinsed
6 tablespoons raw cacao powder
6 tablespoons raw honey

¼ cup cold-pressed coconut oil
2 tablespoons lucuma powder
1 vanilla bean
Pinch of Himalayan salt
1 tray of ice cubes (around 14 cubes)

PREPARATION Place the water, avocado, cashews, cacao, honey, coconut oil, lucuma, vanilla bean and salt in a blender and blend on high until smooth. Add the ice and blend again. Divide among 2 glasses and enjoy immediately. If you have any leftover (yeah right!), this freezes beautifully into chocolate ice cream.

Pure Pleasures

Lush Lemon Lavender Libation

Say that 10 times fast! Seriously though, this is a classy drink. It kind of makes me feel like an adult—but only kind of! The sophisticated blend of lemon, lavender and mint is a show stopper with its layers of color and depth of flavor. Share this at your next toast-worthy occasion. Your guests will be totally impressed and with the high vibration, no one will be missing the alcohol buzz.

Serves 10

Lavender Lemon Juice
½ cup fresh lemon juice
3 tablespoons dried lavender flowers

Candied Lemon Syrup
1 cup raw honey **or** raw agave nectar
½ cup fresh lemon juice
4 teaspoons lemon zest

To serve
40 oz sparkling water
40 mint leaves, crushed
Lemon slices, for garnish
Lots of ice

Lavender Lemon Juice Soak the lavender in lemon juice for 4 hours. Once done, the color is unbelievable! Strain. Save the lavender for garnishing.

Candied Lemon Syrup Blend the honey, lemon juice and zest to create your syrup.

Per Serving Fill a 12 oz glass with ice. Add in 4 crushed mint leaves. Cover with 4 oz of sparkling water. Stir in 2 tablespoons candy lemon syrup. Top with 2 teaspoons lavender lemon juice and let your guests mix their own so they can see the beautiful layered color effect. Garnish with a few lavender buds and a slice of lemon. Watch as your guests sip in bliss!

Pure Pleasures

ELECTRIC LEMONADE

Lemonade has always been a favorite spring and summer drink for me and my family. Sure, I drink lots of pure water, but when the weather starts to warm up and I am drinking more and more, I like to add in some other creative ways to quench my thirst. Lemon is an amazing body cleanser and packs a high vitamin C punch. Sweetened with raw honey and jazzed up with fresh mint & ginger, you will be fully energized & inspired to get out into nature and enjoy a beautiful day!

Serves 2

INGREDIENTS
2 cups pure water
Juice and pulp of 2 lemons
2 tablespoons mint leaves
½" cube of fresh ginger, peeled
3 tablespoons raw honey

PREPARATION Place all ingredients in a blender and blend on high to combine. Fill 2 large glasses with ice, if desired. Pour over ice and garnish with additional lemon slices and mint.

GET YOUR TEMPLE GLOWING GREEN JUICE

My favorite way to start the day, hands down. Pure nutrition + fresh green flavor = a happy me and now, a happy YOU! Now if only I could find someone to clean my juicer when I'm done…any takers?

Serves 1

INGREDIENTS
1 green apple, cored
1 large cucumber
½ of a zucchini
6 stalks of celery
6 kale leaves
¼ lemon, with the peel
2" of turmeric **or** 1" of ginger, peeled
1 handful of fresh mint

PREPARATION Run all ingredients through your juicer. Drink immediately. Feel the instant pleasure.

Pure Pleasures

PINEAPPLE CUCUMBER MINT JUICE

A super cooling drink for a hot summer day. This is so yummy! Always keep a pineapple ripening on your counter and mint growing in your herb garden so you can make it in an instant.

Serves 2

INGREDIENTS
1 pineapple, peeled, and cut to fit your juicer (no need to core!)
1 large handful fresh mint
2 medium cucumbers

PREPARATION Run all ingredients through your juicer in the order listed above. Drink immediately & bask in cool bliss.

BALI ELIXIR

Picture this: You are relaxing in paradise, indulging in the best massage of your life. Four hands working in tandem and tropical rains pouring down outside the hut. As the finale, you're served a warm, spicy, exotic drink. This is a true story, and this drink is inspired by one of the pleasures of my life.

Serves 2

INGREDIENTS

1 oz piece of fresh turmeric (3" x ½" piece, peeled)
  or substitute ¾ teaspoon dried turmeric
Juice and pulp of 2 lemons

¼ cup raw honey
2 cups pure water

PREPARATION
Blend all ingredients. Serve on ice if desired. Proceed to daydream excessively or just book your exotic vacation for real, like now.

RASPBERRY LIME RICKEY

My family and I used to love this cute little diner, where we would drink Lime Rickeys full of sugary syrups and tangy flavors. I loved creating this natural version, just as sweet and full of pleasure as the ones I drank as a kid, but now made with ingredients I can feel great about putting into my pure body.

Serves 2

INGREDIENTS
1 cup pure water
¾ cup freshly squeezed lime juice
6 tablespoons raw honey
8 oz raspberry flavored kombucha
Crushed ice

PREPARATION Blend water, lime juice and honey until well combined. Fill two 16 oz glasses ⅓ of the way with crushed ice. Divide the lime mixture over the two ice filled glasses. Top each off with 4 oz of kombucha. Mix if desired, but I love to leave it and watch the way the colors layer. Drink and giggle like when you were little.

Pure Pleasures

Piña Verde

Green Smoothies rock my world. My blender is super simple to clean, so a lot of times, instead of juicing, I blend my greens with fruit. This green smoothie has a bit of an island feel with the pineapple and lime. Make it, drink it, love it!

Serves 1

Ingredients
2½ cups pineapple
½ cup cilantro
Juice from ½ small lime

PREPARATION Place all ingredients in a blender and blend on high until smooth. Drink immediately & enjoy!

Florida Citrus Green Smoothie

I have deep rooted wanderlust, but at this moment, I'm calling Florida home. I grew up in New England, so the idea of fresh, local fruit being available in the winter is beyond exciting to me! I've got lemons, limes & tangerines growing right in my very own yard. Woo hoo! Even if you have to buy your citrus, this is still worth making for an energizing breakfast or snack.

Serves 1

Ingredients
Juice of 4 small oranges
2 apples, cored & roughly chopped
1 lemon, peeled, seeded and cut into quarters
2 stalks of celery, with leaves
8 kale leaves

PREPARATION Place all ingredients in a blender and blend on high until smooth. Enjoy a little taste of where I call home.

Pure Pleasures

SOUR GREEN GRAPE

Grapes make the perfect sweet, juicy base for green smoothies. Whenever I have grapes in the house, they're usually quickly gone to snacking, but if I can think fast, this delicious green smoothie is mine.

Serves 1

INGREDIENTS
2½ cups green grapes
3 cups of spinach
Juice of 2 limes

PREPARATION Place all ingredients in a blender and blend on high until smooth.

SAVORY GREEN SMOOTHIE

Sometimes I'm just not up for something super sweet and my body asks for savory, salty, green goodness. This can be served up as a soup or smoothie, however you prefer to drink it down.

Serves 1-2

INGREDIENTS
1 cup pure water
4 stalks of celery with leaves
1 avocado
1 medium cucumber
1 lemon, peeled and seeded
1 handful of parsley
1 clove of garlic
¼ teaspoon Himalayan salt

PREPARATION Place all ingredients in a blender and blend on high until smooth. Pour into a bowl or glass and enjoy a pure green moment.

Pure Pleasures

Strawberry Mango Lime Smoothie

Simply sweet…with a little kiss of lime!

Serves 1

Ingredients

1¼ cup strawberries
1 cup mango
3 tablespoons lime juice
2 tablespoons raw honey

PREPARATION Blend all ingredients and drink up to your heart's content.

PEACHES & BLUEBERRY CREAM

Peaches and blueberries make a luscious combination when blended with a sweet vanilla cream. Serve it as a breakfast or dessert—or better yet, as dessert for breakfast. Now that's pure pleasure!

Serves 2

INGREDIENTS

1½ cups pure water
¼ cup raw cashews, soaked 1 hour, drained/rinsed
3 Medjool dates, pitted

1 vanilla bean
4 ripe peaches, pitted
1 cup blueberries

PREPARATION Blend the water, cashews, dates, and vanilla bean until smooth. Add the peaches and blueberries and blend again. Add a little ice if you prefer a chilled smoothie. Drink up!

SUNDAY BREAKFAST

For me, breakfast is usually a quick juice or smoothie. When I have a little more time on the weekends, I reminisce about the big Sunday breakfasts I used to share with my family while growing up. When I am really craving a special wake up, I will prepare something that takes me back and really fulfills me in body, mind & spirit.

Banana Walnut Muffin Tops

Muffins are an "OMG give me comfort food right now please & thank you very much" kind of food. Keep these on hand for those days.

Makes 2 dozen

INGREDIENTS

2½ cups raw walnuts, soaked 4-6 hours, drained/rinsed
5 ripe bananas
¼ cup mesquite powder
¾ cup raw honey
3 tablespoons cinnamon

Seeds of 1 vanilla bean
½ teaspoon nutmeg
⅛ teaspoon cloves
Pinch of Himalayan salt
¼ cup ground flax seeds

PREPARATION Place 2 cups of the walnuts in the food processor and process into a paste. Add 3 of the bananas, mesquite, honey, cinnamon, vanilla, nutmeg, cloves and salt to the food processor. Process until a sticky dough forms. Add the flax and process one more time until well combined. Scrape into a bowl. Roughly chop the remaining 2 bananas and mix into the dough. For each muffin, place 2 heaping tablespoons of batter onto nonstick dehydrator sheets and press into circles about ½" thick. Roughly chop the remaining ½ cup walnuts and evenly sprinkle over the tops. Press in slightly so they stick into the batter. Dehydrate at 145° for 2 hours, then for an additional 6-8 hours at 115°. Flip over and remove the nonstick sheets. Continue to dehydrate for 12-14 hours until dry, but still soft and sticky. Store in the refrigerator. Feel calmed and comforted while enjoying with a cup of tea.

Pure Pleasures

LAVENDER CREAM BLINTZES WITH BLACKBERRY SYRUP

Seriously—wow, this is out of control good. Well worth the time and effort. Even worth buying a dehydrator for (if you don't have one). What else can I say? Indulge in every sweet bite.

Makes 16

BLINTZ WRAPS
3 small apples
2 teaspoons lemon juice
1 cup shredded coconut
1 teaspoon cinnamon
¼ cup raw honey
6 tablespoons cold-pressed coconut oil
¼ teaspoon vanilla extract
⅛ teaspoon nutmeg
Pinch of Himalayan salt
⅓ cup ground flax seeds
⅔ cup pure water

LAVENDER CREAM
½ cup pure water
¾ cup coconut butter*
1 vanilla bean
¼ cup raw honey
1¼ cup raw macadamia nuts, soaked 4-6 hours, drained/rinsed
2 teaspoons dried lavender

BLACKBERRY SYRUP
1½ cups blackberries
6 tablespoons raw honey

BLINTZ WRAPS Peel the apples and cut them into quarters. Remove the cores. Using the shredding disc of your food processor, shred the apples. You should have approximately 1¾ cups of apple after shredding. Toss immediately in a large bowl with the lemon juice to prevent browning. Add the coconut, cinnamon, honey, coconut oil, vanilla, nutmeg and salt to the bowl and mix well. In a separate bowl, whisk together the flax seeds and water. Once there are no remaining lumps, add this to the apple mixture and mix very well. Prepare your dehydrator trays with nonstick sheets. For each wrap, scoop 2 tablespoons of batter onto the tray. Spread into even circles around 4-5" in diameter. Continue until all batter is used. Dehydrate at 105° for 4-6 hours. Flip over and remove the nonstick sheets. Continue to dehydrate for another 6-8 hours until dry, but still very flexible. Store at room temperature. For longer storage you may keep these in the refrigerator, but be sure to return to room temperature to regain their flexibility.

LAVENDER CREAM Place all ingredients except for the lavender in a high-speed blender and blend from low to high. Once your cream is very smooth, add the lavender and blend gently until combined. Pour into a glass container and chill in the refrigerator.

Pure Pleasures

BLACKBERRY SYRUP Blend the blackberries and honey until smooth.

ASSEMBLY Begin with a wrap and place 2 tablespoons of cream in the center. Spread the cream so that it runs in a vertical line from one end of the circle to another. Roll up, keeping the cream running vertically in the center of the wrap. Arrange so that the seam is at the bottom of the wrap and place on a plate. Drizzle generously with blackberry syrup and serve…perhaps as breakfast in bed.

If you do not have access to coconut butter, you can substitute ½ cup coconut oil and an additional ¼ cup macadamia nuts.

SUPER SEED BREAD & CHIVE CREAM CHEESE

Bagels & cream cheese, oh how I love thee…I love live food, but when I made the switch from cooked to raw, I was desperate for something to fulfill this craving—like I couldn't live without it. Okay, that's dramatic, but having this to turn to is deeply satisfying.

Makes 3½ dehydrator trays of bread and 1½ cups of cream cheese

SUPER SEED BREAD

2 small zucchini
2 small apples
2 cups raw sunflower seeds, soaked 4-6 hours, drained/rinsed
¾ cup cold-pressed olive oil
1 cup pure water
½ cup roughly chopped onion
½ cup hemp seeds
½ cup raw sesame seeds
¼ cup chia seeds
2 tablespoons poppy seeds
2 tablespoons caraway seeds
1½ teaspoons Himalayan salt
1 cup ground flax seeds

CHIVE CREAM CHEESE

1½ cups raw cashews, soaked 1 hour, drained/rinsed
¼ cup pure water
¼ cup lemon juice
¾ teaspoon Himalayan salt
½ teaspoon chickpea miso
¼ cup fresh chives, minced

SUPER SEED BREAD Peel the zucchini. Using the shredding disc of the food processor, shred the zucchini. Scrape into a large bowl. You should have 1½ cups of shredded zucchini. Peel and core the apples. Shred the apple in the food processor. You should have 1¼ cups of shredded apple. Pour into the bowl with the zucchini. Process the sunflower seeds until well ground. Add to the bowl. Process the onions until finely chopped but not pureed. Add to the bowl. Add the olive oil, water, onion, hemp, sesame, chia, poppy, caraway seeds and salt to the bowl. Mix very well. Add the flax seeds last, mixing very well to ensure there are no lumps. Prepare 4 dehydrator trays with nonstick sheets. Place 2 cups of batter on each tray. Spread the dough evenly to the edges of the trays. Place the trays in the dehydrator at 145° for 90 minutes. After 90 minutes, turn the temperature down to 105°. After 4 hours, flip the bread onto the mesh dehydrator sheets and remove nonstick sheets. Dehydrate for an additional 10-12 hours. Once done, place the bread on a cutting board and cut into desired shapes.

Pure Pleasures

CHIVE CREAM CHEESE Place all ingredients except for the chives in a high-speed blender and blend on high until smooth and creamy. Scrape into a bowl and fold in the chives. Chill in the refrigerator. Spread chilled cream cheese on Super Seed Bread and top with additional veggies if desired. I love adding slices of fresh, ripe tomatoes. Bagel & cream cheese crisis averted.

FRUITY CHIA PUDDING

This is so lovely, like tapioca pearls in a sweet vanilla cream with the freshest of fruit. The chia seeds will absorb the liquid and plump up to thicken it into a pudding. Plus, chia is super filling and totally keeps you going until lunchtime.

Serves 4

INGREDIENTS
2 cups pure water
⅓ cup raw cashews
4-6 pitted Medjool dates **or** sweetener of choice
2 vanilla beans
1 teaspoon lucuma powder (optional)
Pinch of Himalayan salt
5-6 tablespoons chia seeds
2 cups of fresh fruit, I love berries, peaches and mangos

PREPARATION In a high-speed blender, combine the water, cashews, sweetener, vanilla, lucuma and salt. Blend until smooth. Pour into a bowl and whisk in the chia seeds. Begin with 5 tablespoons. Let stand for 15 minutes to thicken. Stir to break up any clumps and add an additional tablespoon of chia if you feel you want a thicker pudding. I like mine a little on the runny side. When it's to your liking, stir in 2 cups of fresh fruit and serve. I love to eat this on my porch on a warm day.

Pure Pleasures

SMALL BITES

For me, life is a bunch of small meals spread throughout the day. Everything is so nutrient dense and filling. It is a salad here, a wrap there, a piece of fruit a bit later and of course, something sweet everyday. So although these may traditionally be served as appetizers, snacks or sides, feel free to turn them into lunch or dinner like I enjoy doing.

SPICY CITRUS BROCCOLI

I used to make less healthful choices when it came to Chinese food. Now I reach for fresh, crunchy veggies and homemade, flavorful sauces. In this dish, broccoli and red pepper are tossed in a zesty orange sauce. With sesame, ginger, and chili, this dish is bursting with Eastern inspired flavor. If you have a dehydrator available, you may try dehydrating the finished dish to soften and warm the broccoli. You will certainly enjoy it either way! This would be fabulous served along side Chive Rangoons (page 34).

Serves 4 as a side dish

SPICY CITRUS SAUCE
3 tablespoons raw sesame tahini
2 tablespoons coconut aminos
2 tablespoons cold–pressed sesame oil
1 tablespoon raw honey **or** raw agave nectar
2 cloves of garlic, minced
1 teaspoon grated orange zest
¼ teaspoon grated ginger
¼ teaspoon crushed chili pepper
¼ teaspoon Himalayan salt

VEGGIES
2½ cups broccoli florets, very thinly sliced
½ cup diced red bell pepper
2 small scallions, very thinly sliced

GARNISH
3 tablespoons raw sesame seeds, divided

PREPARATION Place all ingredients for the Spicy Citrus Sauce into a large bowl and whisk well until smooth. Add the broccoli, bell pepper and scallions to the sauce and toss well to coat. Sprinkle with 2 tablespoons of sesame seeds and mix again. If you choose to dehydrate, spread the entire mixture on a dehydrator tray lined with a nonstick sheet. Dehydrate at 105° for 3 hours. Divide among 4 plates and sprinkle with the remaining sesame seeds to garnish.

Pure Pleasures

SESAME GINGER LETTUCE WRAPS

This is a great dish to make as a raw food first impression. The first time I made them, I couldn't stop eating. These wraps are so full of flavor, whenever I serve them, the compliments are flying at me. Give it a go!

Makes 24 wraps

WRAPS
2 heads Butter lettuce
¼ cup black sesame seeds for garnish

SESAME GINGER CRUMBLE
3 cups raw walnuts, soaked 4-6 hours, drained/rinsed and dehydrated 12-24 hours*
3 tablespoons sweet onion, minced
3 tablespoons coconut aminos
1 tablespoon raw honey **or** raw agave nectar
1 tablespoon cold-pressed sesame oil
1 clove of garlic, minced
1 teaspoon fresh ginger, grated
Pinch of cayenne, to taste

GINGER MARINATED VEGGIES
½ green cabbage, finely shredded
¼ teaspoon Himalayan salt
2 carrots, shredded
¼ bunch cilantro leaves, lightly chopped
3 scallions, finely chopped
¼ cup lime juice
¼ cup + 2 tablespoons cold-pressed sesame oil
2 tablespoons coconut aminos
3 tablespoons raw honey **or** raw agave nectar
1 teaspoon grated ginger
1 clove of garlic

SESAME GINGER CRUMBLE Pulse the walnuts in the food processor until they are coarsely ground. Whisk all remaining ingredients together in a large bowl. Add the walnuts and toss well to coat.

GINGER MARINATED VEGGIES Place the cabbage in a large bowl and sprinkle with salt. Massage the salt into the cabbage a bit with your hands to encourage it to soften and wilt. Toss the cabbage with the carrot, cilantro and scallions. Combine remaining ingredients in a bowl and whisk well. Pour this dressing over your cabbage mixture and toss. Mix with your hands to further soften the cabbage.

Pure Pleasures

ASSEMBLY Start with a leaf of Butter lettuce. Top with ¼ cup of the Sesame Ginger Crumble. Cover with ¼ cup of Ginger Marinated Veggies. Sprinkle with sesame seeds. Repeat for all remaining wraps. You and your guests will be very pleased with the result!

Feel free to substitute Brazil nuts if you have not prepared walnuts, as Brazil nuts do not require soaking or dehydrating.

CHIVE RANGOONS

I always loved the greasiest Chinese food I could get my hands on and I was completely Crab Rangoon obsessed! This recipe, almost unbelievably, completely satisfies that long time craving. Prepare to have your socks knocked off!

Makes 15 pieces

WONTON WRAPPERS
2 medium zucchini
1 cup shredded coconut
2 tablespoons coconut aminos
¼ cup cold-pressed coconut oil
2 tablespoons cold-pressed sesame oil
3 scallions, green parts only, finely chopped
⅓ cup ground flax seeds
⅔ cup pure water

CHIVE CREAM
1½ cup raw cashews, soaked 1 hour, drained/rinsed
¼ cup pure water
¼ cup lemon juice
¾ teaspoon Himalayan salt
½ teaspoon miso
¼ cup fresh chives, minced
¼ cup red pepper, minced
1 large clove of garlic, minced

GINGER DIPPING SAUCE
¼ cup coconut aminos
1 tablespoon cold-pressed sesame oil
2 teaspoons raw honey **or** raw agave nectar
1 teaspoon umeboshi vinegar
1 teaspoon ginger, grated
1 teaspoon raw sesame seeds
¼ teaspoon crushed chili pepper
Chopped scallions for garnish

WONTON WRAPPERS Peel the zucchini. Using the shredding disc of the food processor, shred the zucchini. Scrape into a large bowl. You should have 1¾ cups of shredded zucchini.   Mix in the coconut, coconut aminos, coconut oil, sesame oil and scallions. In a separate bowl, whisk together flax seeds and water. Add the flax mixture to the larger bowl and mix everything well. Prepare 3 dehydrator trays with nonstick sheets. For each wrap, drop 2 tablespoons of batter onto the tray and spread into an even circle that is around 4-5" in diameter. Dehydrate for 4-6 hours at 105°. Flip over and remove the nonstick sheets. Continue to dehydrate for another 6-8 hours until crisp, but flexible.

Pure Pleasures

CHIVE CREAM Place the cashews, water, lemon juice, salt and miso in a high-speed blender and blend until smooth and creamy. Scrape into a bowl and fold in the chives, red pepper and garlic.

GINGER DIPPING SAUCE Whisk all ingredients together in a small bowl.

ASSEMBLY For each rangoon, lay one wrap on a plate. Spread on 2 tablespoons of the chive cream filling to cover the entire wrap. Fold in half creating a half circle filled with cream. Serve with ginger dipping sauce on the side.

SEVEN LAYER TACO DIP

I'll be the first to admit to the ridiculousness of this recipe. I recommend dividing the prep duties between friends. It's so worth it! Think about serving this up at a party and watching everyone's jaws drop. This one goes out to my girl Kate—totally her idea to give a raw version of her favorite party dip a try. If you're not up for making all layers at once, but still want some yummy live Mexican food, combine a few of the layers to make burritos or tacos wrapped in lettuce.

Fills one 9" round spring form pan to the top!

LAYER 1. CHIPOTLE BEANS

2 cups raw sunflower seeds, soaked 4-6 hours, drained/rinsed
½ cup sun dried tomatoes, soaked 4-6 hours in pure water, drained
¼ cup cold-pressed olive oil
1 tablespoon lime juice
2 cloves of garlic
2 tablespoons chili powder
1 teaspoon ground chipotle
2 teaspoons cumin
½ teaspoon Himalayan salt
½ cup pure water
3 scallions, minced

CHIPOTLE BEANS Process all ingredients except scallions until smooth and creamy. Pour into a bowl and mix in the scallions by hand.

LAYER 2. RED PEPPER QUESO

2 tablespoons lemon juice
2 tablespoons pure water
½ cup red bell pepper, chopped
1 clove of garlic
½ teaspoon Himalayan salt
1 cup raw pine nuts
2 tablespoons cold-pressed olive oil
½ of a small jalapeño, seeded and minced

RED PEPPER QUESO Place the lemon, water, bell pepper, garlic and salt in the blender. Blend well. Add pine nuts and blend again from low to high until smooth and creamy. With the blender still running, add olive oil until just combined. Pour into a bowl and mix in jalapeño by hand.

LAYER 3. TACO CRUMBLE

¼ cup coconut aminos
¼ cup diced onion
3 cups of raw Brazil nuts
4 teaspoons cumin
1 teaspoon oregano
2 teaspoons ground coriander
¼ teaspoon ground chipotle
3 tablespoons cilantro leaves, chopped

TACO CRUMBLE Place the coconut aminos and the onion in a small bowl to marinate. Process the Brazil nuts in a food processor until crumbly. Place the nuts in a larger bowl and toss with spices and cilantro. Pour marinated onion and aminos over the nuts and toss well to combine.

LAYER 4. SUNNY SOUR CREAM

1 cup raw sunflower seeds, soaked 4-6 hours, drained/rinsed
½ cup pure water
¼ cup lemon juice
½ teaspoon Himalayan salt
¼ cup cold-pressed olive oil

SUNNY SOUR CREAM Add all ingredients except olive oil to a high-speed blender and blend from low to high until smooth and creamy. With the blender still running, add olive oil until just combined.

LAYER 5. GUACAMOLE

3 ripe Hass avocados
Juice of one lime
¼ teaspoon Himalayan salt
1 clove of garlic
¼ cup cilantro leaves
½ of a jalapeño, seeded
3 tablespoons chopped onion

GUACAMOLE In a medium sized bowl, mash the avocado, lime and salt with a fork. In a food processor, chop the garlic, cilantro and jalapeño. Add this mixture to the mashed avocado. Chop the onion by hand and add it to the dish. Mix well.

Continued on next page

LAYER 6. SALSA FRESCA

3 medium tomatoes, diced
¼ cup cilantro, chopped
3 tablespoons onion, diced
2 cloves of garlic, minced
1 teaspoon lime juice
¾ teaspoon Himalayan salt
1 teaspoon jalapeño, minced

SALSA FRESCA Mix all ingredients together in a medium sized bowl.

LAYER 7. TOPPING

10 sun dried black olives sliced
2 scallions, minced

ASSEMBLY Layer all ingredients in a 9" round spring form pan in the order listed above. Refrigerate to set.
Remove the sides of the pan when ready to serve. Be prepared to impress! Serve with Purple Corn Chips (*page 47*)
or with lettuce leaves for wrapping.

TROPI-KALE STUFFED AVOCADOS

I love all things kale and avocado! It's one of my favorite combinations: salty, massaged kale and rich, creamy avocado. My body loves a good daily dose of healthy fat to feel full and satisfied. That's how I roll.

Serves 4

INGREDIENTS

2 cups Lacinato kale, thinly sliced
¼ teaspoon Himalayan salt
Juice of one lime
1 tablespoon cold-pressed coconut oil
1 clove of garlic, minced
½ cup diced pineapple

¼ cup diced red bell pepper
2 tablespoons chopped cilantro
2 tablespoons chopped scallions
⅛ teaspoon ground chipotle
2 avocados

PREPARATION
Toss the kale and salt in a large bowl. Massage the kale by hand, encouraging it to soften and wilt. Proceed for several minutes until the kale is very soft. Add the lime juice, coconut oil and garlic and massage a bit more to flavor the kale. Toss in the pineapple, bell pepper, cilantro, scallions and chipotle. Mix very well. Cut your avocados in half and remove the pit. If the hole left by the pit is very small, you may wish to scoop out a bit of the flesh to make room for the stuffing. Divide the kale mixture into four equal portions and fill the avocados. Serve immediately. If you wish to prepare the kale salad in advance, just keep the avocados whole until ready to serve to prevent browning.

THREE-HERB PESTO CANAPÉS

I love so much about this recipe! It is easy, but super impressive, raw but very gourmet and of course, totally delicious! This is a wonderful appetizer to showcase what is growing in your herb garden. The combination of cucumber and fresh herbs is so cool and refreshing. Serve them up at your next hot party!

Makes 3 dozen

THREE-HERB PESTO
3 cloves of garlic
1 cup parsley leaves, well packed
½ cup mint leaves, well packed
1 tablespoon thyme leaves, well packed
¼ cup lemon juice
½ teaspoon lemon zest
¾ teaspoon Himalayan salt
1 cup cold-pressed olive oil
1 cup raw sesame seeds

CANAPÉS
2 medium cucumbers
9 cherry tomatoes
9 sun dried black olives, pitted
36 small sprigs of thyme

THREE-HERB PESTO Place the garlic cloves in a food processor fit with the S-blade. Process to chop. Add the parsley, mint, thyme, lemon juice, lemon zest and salt. Process to finely chop the herbs. Scrape down the sides of the food processor. Add the olive oil and sesame seeds and process once again until well combined.

CANAPÉS Wash the cucumbers and peel if waxed. Or, peel a full-length strip every ½" to make a decorative pattern. Cut into ¼" thick rounds. Slice each cherry tomato into 4 even rounds. Slice each olive into 4 even rounds. Pick out your 36 best, most evenly sized, cucumber rounds. Top each cucumber with 2 teaspoons of Three-Herb Pesto. Place a cherry tomato slice on top of the pesto. Top the cherry tomato with an olive slice. Place a tiny sprig of thyme inside of each olive to garnish your canapés. Place the finished canapés neatly on a platter. Serve and enjoy your fancy party platter!

Heirloom Tomato Stacks
with avocado and cilantro infused oil
....

With just a few simple ingredients, you can have a gourmet dish ready in minutes. Fresh heirloom tomatoes paired with creamy, ripe avocados, refreshing lime and a zesty cilantro infused oil, this Mexican inspired dish makes a delicious starter, side or small meal.

Serves 4

Cilantro Infused Oil
3 cloves of garlic
¾ cup cilantro leaves, well packed
½ cup cold-pressed olive oil
¼ teaspoon Himalayan salt
⅛ teaspoon crushed chili pepper

Stacks
4 heirloom tomatoes of varying color
2 avocados
2 limes

CILANTRO INFUSED OIL Place the peeled garlic cloves in a food processor and pulse to chop. Add the cilantro and process until finely chopped. Scrape the garlic and cilantro into a small bowl. Stir in the olive oil, salt and chili pepper. Set aside.

STACKS Slice the tomatoes into ½" thick slices. For each stack you will need 3 tomato slices. Pick out the 12 most evenly sized slices and mix up the colors for variety. Cut the avocados in half and remove the pits. Each stack will use ½ of an avocado, divided among 3 layers. Slice each avocado thinly, about ¼" per slice. Cut the limes in half.

ASSEMBLY Gather 4 small plates. Place one tomato slice on each plate. Top with a layer of avocado, a generous squeeze of lime juice and a drizzle of Cilantro Infused Oil. Repeat for two more layers, finishing each plate with 3 layers of tomato, avocado, lime and Cilantro Infused Oil. Serve immediately. Indulge with great pleasure!

Pure Pleasures

PESTO-AVOCADO WRAPS

My hubby Adam and I never seem to have enough time. When he is rushing to get ready for work, I am flying around the kitchen, making sure he is going to be well fed for the day with breakfast, lunch & snacks. He is on this raw journey with me, but that doesn't mean he has acquired any new kitchen skills. Some people just don't resonate with food preparation. We have a pretty sweet deal, though. I do what I love, making lots of food in the kitchen (meaning a huge mess) and he cleans up. With such busy lives, it is so important to have tasty & healthy dishes you can throw together in five minutes. I love the idea that Adam is getting a surprise lunch that I often pack when he is in the shower. During the workday, I will get texts like "just had lunch, soooooo good". That makes the morning rush so worth it. This is one of those quick recipes. As long as you have prepped your pesto ahead of time, you will be good to go—fast!

Serves 2

INGREDIENTS

4 lettuce leaves
1 medium tomato, chopped
1 avocado, chopped

1 tablespoon onion, diced
¼ cup Hemp Seed & Basil Pesto (*page 68*)
A handful of micro greens **or** sprouts, for garnishing

PREPARATION Wash and dry your lettuce leaves. Place two on each plate. In a medium bowl, toss together the tomato, avocado, onion and pesto. Divide this filling evenly over the lettuce leaves. Top with micro greens or sprouts. Enjoy immediately or pack for lunch.

Tomato Basil Flatbread

I need dehydrated textures to fulfill that bread/cracker/chip hole in my heart. Life is much more pleasurable when I include things like this. I love little meals of breads, dips and veggies. This is amazing topped with Sunny Hummus (page 72) or Hemp Seed & Basil Pesto (page 68).

Makes 5 full dehydrator trays

Ingredients

2½ cups raw sunflower seeds,
    soaked 4-6 hours, drained/rinsed
4 medium tomatoes, cut in half and sliced very thin
1 cup cold-pressed olive oil
½ cup basil chiffonade (very thinly sliced), well packed
8 cloves of garlic, minced

2 tablespoons oregano
2 teaspoons Himalayan salt
1 cup pure water
3 cups ground flax seeds
5 tablespoons hemp seeds

Preparation

Place the sunflower seeds in a food processor fit with the S-blade. Process well. Scrape into a large bowl. Add tomatoes, olive oil, basil, garlic, oregano, salt and water. Mix very well. Add the flax seeds and mix again until there are no lumps remaining. Divide the batter evenly among 5 dehydrator trays lined with nonstick sheets, using about 1½ cups batter per tray. Spread evenly to the edges. Sprinkle the tops of each tray with 1 tablespoon of hemp seeds. Gently press to set the hemp seeds into the batter. Dehydrate for 90 minutes at 145°. Turn the temperature down to 105° and dehydrate for another 4-6 hours. Flip, peel off the nonstick sheets and continue to dehydrate until fully dry, about 10-12 hours.

Scallion Ginger Almonds & Seeds

This is a sweet and savory Asian inspired snack that is full of flavor & nutrition. I like to keep some in my purse as I never know when I might need a protein packed pick me up…as in, I am out and about, there is nothing around to eat, I am getting cranky and need a pleasure fix!

Makes 8 cups

Ingredients

4 cups raw almonds, soaked 12 hours
2 cups raw sunflower seeds, soaked 4 hours
1½ cups raw pumpkin seeds, soaked 4 hours
½ cup raw sesame seeds
¾ cup coconut aminos
¼ cup raw honey

1 teaspoon fresh grated ginger
4 cloves of garlic, minced
3 scallions, finely chopped
½ teaspoon Himalayan salt
¼ teaspoon cayenne pepper

Preparation

Drain and rinse your almonds and seeds. Place in a very large bowl and toss with the sesame seeds. In a separate, smaller bowl, combine coconut aminos, honey, ginger, garlic, scallions, salt and cayenne. Whisk together to create your marinade. Pour over the almond and seed mixture and toss very well to coat. If time allows, place in the refrigerator and allow to marinate for 12 hours (otherwise you may proceed to dehydrating). After marinating, drain out the liquid. Divide the almond and seed mix equally over 5 mesh dehydrator trays. Dehydrate at 110° for 24 hours. After 24 hours, toss the nuts a bit and dehydrate another 6-12 hours until very dry and crisp.

PURPLE CORN CHIPS

yum, Yum, YUM! Crunchy purple corn chips that you are going to love to have on hand when you've got salsa, guacamole, or better yet, the Seven Layer Taco Dip (page 36).

Makes 4 full dehydrator trays

INGREDIENTS

1½ cups dried purple corn kernels
3 cups pure water
1 cup raw sunflower seeds, soaked 4-6 hours, drained/rinsed
1¾ cups red bell pepper, chopped
⅓ cup onion
1 teaspoons cumin
2½ teaspoons Himalayan salt

1½ teaspoons lime juice
1 clove of garlic
½ cup ground flax seeds
½ cup whole flax
1 cup black sesame seeds
Additional salt for sprinkling

PREPARATION

Blend the purple corn kernels and water in a high-speed blender until smooth. Add remaining ingredients except flax and sesame seeds to the blender and blend again until well combined. Pour into a bowl. Add ground and whole flax seeds and sesame seeds to the bowl. Whisk well to remove any lumps. Prepare your dehydrator trays with nonstick sheets. Divide the batter among 4 trays and spread thinly. Dehydrate at 115° for 4 hours. Flip over and remove the nonstick sheets. Sprinkle the tops with salt and score with a knife or pizza cutter into desired shapes. Dehydrate for an additional 10-12 hours or until crisp. Break on the score lines. Get your dip on.

SASSY SALADS

When I first got into live foods, I figured I would be eating a lot of salad; though I was not aware of just how much pleasure a simple salad would bring me. My body just craves these crunchy, green, beautifully dressed bowls full of goodness. The possibilities of salad creations are limitless. I encourage you to have fun tossing up your favorite veggies, fruits & dressings. These are some of my favorite combinations that I just can't get enough of.

ROMANESCO & FRENCH BEANS IN PARSLEY PESTO

Romanesco, a cauliflower relative, is so strikingly beautiful! The sacred geometry of this plant alone is reason enough to purchase and display it as part of a centerpiece. The flavor is slightly milder than traditional cauliflower and is quite nice raw. It shines in this salad along with green beans, scallions and cherry tomatoes. Tossed with a lemony parsley pesto, you will be thrilled that you gave this new vegetable a try. If you have trouble locating it, feel free to substitute broccoli or cauliflower.

Serves 4

PARSLEY PESTO
3 cloves of garlic
Zest of one lemon
6 cups flat leaf parsley (loosely packed)
½ cup cold-pressed olive oil
1 cup raw walnuts, soaked 4-6 hours, drained/rinsed
   and dehydrated 12-24 hours
¾ teaspoon Himalayan salt
½ teaspoon freshly ground black pepper

ROMANESCO SALAD
2 cups thinly sliced Romanesco
1 cup French (green) beans, bias cut to 1" in length
¾ cup sliced cherry tomatoes
½ cup chopped scallions

PARSLEY PESTO Place the garlic cloves in a food processor fit with the S-blade. Process to chop. Add the lemon zest and parsley and process again. You may need to process the parsley 1 cup at a time depending on the capacity of your food processor. Add all remaining ingredients and process until all of the nuts have been finely chopped and all ingredients are well combined.

ROMANESCO SALAD Prepare all of your salad veggies and toss in a large bowl. Pour the Parsley Pesto over the veggies and toss well to coat.

Pure Pleasures

ITALIAN ARTICHOKE TOSS

This is such a pleasant surprise! I love artichoke hearts and I am thrilled to be able to still enjoy them in the raw. This salad has so much flavor with its zesty Italian marinade, fresh herbs, nutty hemp seeds and salty olives. Yes, please!

Serves 4

INGREDIENTS

¼ cup cold-pressed olive oil
2 cloves of garlic, minced
½ teaspoon Himalayan salt
¼ teaspoon crushed chili pepper
¼ cup red onion, sliced into very thin strips on a mandoline
¼ cup chopped parsley, well packed
⅓ cup lemon juice
3 medium artichokes
2 tablespoons hemp seeds
8 Sicilian olives, sliced

PREPARATION Begin by making a marinade, whisking together the olive oil, garlic, salt and chili pepper. Set aside. Prepare the onion and parsley; set aside. Juice the lemons and place remaining rinds in a large bowl of cold water. Prepare the artichokes by removing and discarding all of the sharp outer leaves. Stop when you reach the pale inner leaves. Peel the stem with a vegetable peeler. Place the artichokes in the lemon water bath to prevent browning. Removing one artichoke from the bath at a time, slice the tender parts, including the stem, very finely into thin strips. Remove the fuzzy choke and any sharp inner leaves and discard. Place the sliced artichoke in a large bowl and immediately drench in the lemon juice to prevent browning. Toss with the onion, parsley and the prepared marinade. Mix in the hemp seeds and olives. Top with additional hemp seeds and chili pepper to garnish when serving. Serve immediately.

Pure Pleasures

HARVEST SLAW

This slaw combines the completely underrated celery root with sweet pears in a creamy nut based mayo. It reminds me of the pleasures of my grandmother's potato salad, which of course, is a major comfort food.

Serves 4

HARVEST SLAW
28 oz celery root
2 medium Anjou pears
½ cup red onion, sliced into very thin strips on a mandoline
½ cup raw walnuts, roughly chopped
¼ cup cilantro leaves, chopped
Black pepper to taste

MACADAMIA MAYO
1 cup raw macadamia nuts
½ cup pure water
¼ cup lemon juice
2 cloves of garlic
½ teaspoon mustard seeds
¼ cup cold-pressed olive oil
½ teaspoon Himalayan salt
Black pepper, to taste

HARVEST SLAW Peel the celery root with a knife to remove all of the thick, knobby skin. Cut into a few pieces so that they will fit through the feed tube of your food processor. Shred in the food processor with the proper blade. Core the pears and shred in food processor. Toss the celery root, pear, onion, walnuts and cilantro in a large bowl.

MACADAMIA MAYO Combine all ingredients except olive oil in a high-speed blender. Blend until smooth. With the blender running, add the olive oil slowly to emulsify. Pour the mayo over the Harvest Slaw and mix very well. Serve with freshly ground black pepper.

Pure Pleasures

FRESH HERB & KALE TABBOULEH

Tabbouleh has long been a favorite summer salad in my family. My recipe uses nutrient dense kale along side the classic parsley component for a super green, super healthy & super delicious light meal or side. The fresh mint and thyme make this a very special salad.

Serves 8

TABBOULEH
2 bunches parsley
1 bunch Lacinato kale
¼ teaspoon Himalayan salt
⅓ cup fresh mint leaves
1½ cups halved grape tomatoes
1 cup seeded and diced cucumber
1 cup hemp seeds
½ cup diced sweet onion

DRESSING
½ cup lemon juice
3 cloves of garlic
2 tablespoons sweet onion
1 teaspoon Himalayan salt
½ teaspoon black pepper
⅔ cup cold-pressed olive oil
1 tablespoon fresh thyme leaves

TABBOULEH De-stem all greens. Finely shred the kale and place in a large bowl. Sprinkle with the salt and massage with your hands until it begins to soften and wilt. Finely chop the parsley, either by hand or in a food processor. Add to the bowl. Chop the mint by hand and mix with parsley and kale. Toss in your remaining salad ingredients.

DRESSING Add all ingredients except olive oil and thyme to a blender. Blend until smooth. With the blade running, add the olive oil and thyme last, until just combined. Pour over salad and toss well. Enjoy by the bowlful!

Rainbow Slaw with Chipotle Mayo

I love any version of a cole slaw. This one combines a rainbow of fresh veggies to nourish all of your chakras. The mayo has a mild heat to suit a sensitive palate like mine, so feel free to add more chipotle for those who like a real kick! I love chipotle for its smokiness, which feels like a little raw food naughtiness.

Serves 8

Chipotle Mayo
1 cup raw sunflower seeds, soaked 4-6 hours, drained/rinsed
¾ cup cold-pressed olive oil
⅓ cup pure water
¼ cup lime juice
3 cloves of garlic
1 teaspoon ground chipotle
1 teaspoon Himalayan salt
1 teaspoon cumin
½ teaspoon coriander

Rainbow Slaw
5 cups finely shredded cabbage
1½ cups shredded carrot
1 cup red & yellow bell pepper, julienned
¾ cup red onion, cut into very thin strips
¼ cup chopped cilantro leaves, well packed

CHIPOTLE MAYO Place all ingredients except olive oil in a high-speed blender. Blend until creamy. Add the olive oil last with the blender running until just combined.

RAINBOW SLAW Toss all of your veggies in a very large bowl. Pour the mayo over the slaw and mix very well.

PRETTY IN PINK CUCUMBER-BEET SALAD

Cool cucumber, beets & dill remind me of the cold Russian borscht my grandmother serves every summer…now available in salad form. When you mix it up with the tangy yogurt, this salad is pastel pink—my favorite color.

Serves 6

CUCUMBER-BEET SALAD
2 medium cucumbers
4 small beets, peeled
½ cup dill, chopped and well packed
½ cup sweet or red onion, thinly sliced

YOGURT SAUCE
1 cup raw sunflower seeds, soaked 4-6 hours, drained/rinsed
¼ cup lemon juice
¼ cup pure water
1 clove of garlic
½ teaspoon Himalayan salt
¼ cup cold-pressed olive oil

CUCUMBER-BEET SALAD Using a mandoline, slice the cucumber and beet on the thinnest setting. You should end up with approximately 3 cups of each after slicing. Toss in a large bowl with the dill and onion.

YOGURT SAUCE Add all ingredients except for the olive oil to the blender. Blend until smooth. With the blender still running, add the olive oil and blend until just combined. Pour over your salad and mix well. Alternately, keep the yogurt sauce separate from the salad. Serve the salad with a large dollop of yogurt sauce for each serving to be mixed individually. Garnish with additional dill.

Pure Pleasures

KALE & AVOCADO SALAD

Coming from a former potato chip addict, I never dreamed that I would ever call kale my favorite food. Well, today it is, since learning many versatile ways to prepare it. Here, a light lemon and garlic marinade provide the perfect accompaniment along with hearty chunks of avocado & nutty hemp seeds for a more filling salad. This is on my dinner table at least once a week. The more greens I eat, the more my body craves them and the more pleasure I feel! Give it a try and see if you get the same result: craving greens over junk food!

Serves 2

INGREDIENTS

1 small bunch of Lacinato kale, stems removed
½ teaspoon Himalayan salt
3 tablespoons cold-pressed olive oil
2 tablespoons lemon juice

2 cloves of garlic, minced
2 tablespoons red onion, diced
2 tablespoons hemp seeds
1 ripe avocado, cubed
½ cup cucumber, diced

PREPARATION Stack the kale, a few leaves at a time, and cut into very thin ribbons. Place in a large bowl and sprinkle with ¼ teaspoon of salt. Using your hands, massage the salt into the kale, squeezing and tossing until the kale begins to wilt. Add the olive oil, lemon, garlic and onion to the bowl and continue to massage with your hands as the kale will soften more and shrink down in size. Lastly, add the hemp seeds, avocado and cucumber and toss gently. Taste for salt and add another ¼ teaspoon if desired. Enjoy!

CHEESY GREENS

Like a lot of kids, I grew up on cheese covered food. I was a complete cheese addict and had tons of trouble giving up the ooey gooey goodness. Thank heavens for nuts! They make amazing, creamy sauces to satisfy my cravings. I love this as a salad or warmed from the dehydrator.

Makes 2 hearty servings

CHEESY SAUCE
1 cup raw pine nuts
¼ cup red bell pepper
2 tablespoons lemon juice
2 tablespoons pure water
1 small clove of garlic
¼ teaspoon miso
¼ teaspoon Himalayan salt

GREENS
2 bunches Lacinato kale, stems removed
¼ teaspoon Himalayan salt
¼ cup hemp seeds
Freshly ground black pepper to taste

CHEESY SAUCE Place all ingredients in a high-speed blender and blend until smooth.

GREENS Stack the kale, a few leaves at a time, and cut into very thin ribbons. Place in a large bowl and sprinkle with ¼ teaspoon of salt. Using your hands, massage the salt into the kale, squeezing and tossing until the kale begins to wilt. Pour the Cheesy Sauce over the greens and toss well. Sprinkle with hemp seeds and pepper. If desired, spread the cheesy greens on a dehydrator tray lined with a nonstick sheet. Dehydrate at 105° for 1-2 hours until warm.

GETTING SAUCY

Sauces, dips and dressings are essential elements for live food pleasure. These are what really add satisfaction and fulfillment to my daily meals. They bring salads, wraps and veggies to life with their creamy textures and depth of flavor.

CREAMY PEPPERCORN RANCH DRESSING

This is pretty much my favorite recipe. During my first year on live foods, I lived off of salads covered with this dressing. I tried to keep it as my little secret, but every time I shared a taste with friends, they would nicely ask for the recipe and I could not refuse. This recipe scored me the third place spot in Living Light Culinary Arts Institute's 2010 Hot Raw Chef Contest! It is very nourishing and filling, full of rich creamy goodness. It is also fabulous with crudités, crackers, wraps and sandwiches. Do not be alarmed by the amount of garlic here—the flavors all blend very nicely.

Makes 2¼ cups

INGREDIENTS
⅓ cup pure water
⅓ cup lemon juice
⅔ cup hemp seeds
5 cloves of garlic
2 teaspoons whole black peppercorns
1 teaspoon Himalayan salt
1 cup cold-pressed olive oil

PREPARATION
Place the water, lemon juice, hemp seeds, garlic, peppercorns and salt in a high-speed blender. Blend from low to high speed until smooth. With the blender running on low, pour in the olive oil to emulsify. Gradually turn up the power until just combined. The result should be very thick, creamy & delicious.

Pure Pleasures

Sesame Ginger Dressing

I love wrapping and rolling veggies in big collard, kale or lettuce leaves and covering them in tasty sauces. This Asian inspired dressing is fabulous with wraps full of cabbage, avocado, bell pepper, carrots and sprouts. It also tastes great on thinly sliced broccoli and bok choy.

Makes ½ cup

INGREDIENTS

6 tablespoons cold-pressed sesame oil

2 tablespoons coconut aminos

1 tablespoon raw honey or raw agave nectar

1 tablespoon raw sesame seeds

1 clove of garlic, minced

½ teaspoon grated ginger

½ teaspoon lime zest

¼ teaspoon crushed chili pepper

PREPARATION Whisk all ingredients in a small bowl until well combined. Drizzle generously on your choice of veggies.

CREAMY SPINACH & CILANTRO DIP

I love to challenge myself to create recipes that I can make with completely local ingredients. There are times of the year when I can get everything for this recipe, minus the salt, from local organic farmers. Plus, now I'm growing my own limes…it does not get more local than that!

Makes 1¾ cup

INGREDIENTS

1 large clove of garlic
2 tablespoons chopped onion
½ of a small jalapeño
1 Hass avocado

½ cup cilantro leaves
2 tablespoons lime juice
¼ teaspoon Himalayan salt
2 cups spinach, well packed

PREPARATION Place the garlic, onion, and jalapeño in the food processor and chop finely. Add all other ingredients except for the spinach and process until smooth. Add the spinach and pulse gently until just combined, so that it still retains some texture. Chill until ready to serve. This is delicious with fresh bell pepper spears or Purple Corn Chips (*page 47*).

DILL & ONION DIP

I often mention that I was a potato chip addict right before I made the switch to live food. It was not too uncommon to see me with a big bowl of creamy dip alongside my chips. Now I go for crunchy veggies and flax crackers dipped into flavorful, dairy-free delights like this one.

Makes 2½ cups

INGREDIENTS
¾ cup diced red onion
2 tablespoons coconut aminos
1 cup raw cashews, soaked 1 hour, drained/rinsed
½ cup pure water
¼ cup lemon juice
¼ cup hemp seeds
3 cloves of garlic
¾ teaspoon Himalayan salt
¼ cup cold-pressed olive oil
½ cup of dill, chopped and well packed

PREPARATION Marinate the onion in the coconut aminos for 1 hr. Place on a dehydrator tray lined with a nonstick sheet. Dehydrate at 105° for 6 hours. If a dehydrator is not available, use only ¼ cup diced onion marinated in 2 teaspoons of coconut aminos. Place the cashews, water, lemon juice, hemp seeds, garlic and salt in a blender. Blend until smooth & creamy. With the blender running on low, add the olive oil last to emulsify. Pour into a bowl. Chop the dill finely by hand. Stir the dill and onions into the cream until well mixed. Serve with crudités and flax crackers.

Pure Pleasures

HANDMADE MUSTARD

When my brother Justin told me how easy it was to make mustard, I almost didn't believe him. When I finally gave it a try, I giggled and said I would never buy mustard again. This has a really strong flavor for a true mustard lover (like yours truly). If you like it a little tamer, feel free to mix in more honey or blend with some pine nuts or cashews for a milder and creamier condiment.

Makes 1¾ cups

INGREDIENTS
¾ cup pure water
½ cup raw apple cider vinegar
½ cup yellow mustard seeds
1 teaspoon Himalayan salt
1 tablespoon raw honey
¾ teaspoon onion powder
¾ teaspoon turmeric
½ teaspoon allspice

PREPARATION Combine the water, vinegar, mustard seeds and salt in a glass container with a tight fitting lid. Soak for 48 hours. Once soaked, place in the blender with honey, onion powder, turmeric and allspice. Blend until creamy. Place in the refrigerator for several days to allow the flavor to mellow.

Parsley Pesto

In the heat of a Florida summer, most of the organic farmers take a break. Although I understand, going from huge baskets of dirt cheap, freshly picked produce to the grocery store offerings is a huge shock. I can often find parsley more readily available in larger quantities than basil during this time of year. So, my parsley pesto was born. This is simply delicious with its strong herb flavor and hint of citrus. Use however you would a traditional basil pesto.

Makes 1¼ cups

INGREDIENTS

3 cloves of garlic
Zest of one lemon
6 cups of flat leaf parsley (loosely packed)
½ cup cold-pressed olive oil

1 cup raw walnuts, soaked 4-6 hours, drained/rinsed
  and dehydrated 12-24 hours
¾ teaspoon Himalayan salt
½ teaspoon freshly ground black pepper

PREPARATION Place the garlic cloves in a food processor fit with the S-blade. Process to chop. Add the lemon zest and parsley and process again. You may need to process the parsley 1 cup at a time depending on the capacity of your food processor. Add all remaining ingredients and process until all of the nuts have been finely chopped and all ingredients are well combined. This is really nice on the Tomato Basil Flatbread (*page 45*).

HEMP SEED & BASIL PESTO

Vegan and even raw pestos are not that hard to come by, so I am not trying to say I have invented anything new. I will say, however, this is the best tasting pesto that I have ever had. Using a couple of less traditional ingredients like hemp seeds and miso really give this a surprisingly authentic taste reminiscent of the traditional pine nut and Parmesan ingredients. My amazing friend Wendy insisted that this was better than anything she had tasted in Italy and I took that as the highest of compliments. For that, and for her selfless help in the kitchen over several spring weeks to help me plow through lots of recipes, I dedicate this recipe to Wendy!

I love pesto on anything: tomato slices, flax crackers or breads, cucumbers, zucchini noodles, as a dressing on salads…the sky is truly the limit. Spread generously on Tomato Basil Flatbread (page 45) and top with fresh tomatoes for instant pizza or make the Pesto-Avocado Wraps (page 44).

Makes 1 cup

INGREDIENTS
2 large cloves of garlic
2 cups basil leaves, well packed
½ teaspoon miso
½ teaspoon Himalayan salt
¼ teaspoon black pepper
¾ cup hemp seeds
½ cup cold-pressed olive oil

PREPARATION Process the garlic in your food processor with the S-blade. Scrape down the sides and add the basil to process again. Scrape the sides and then add the miso, salt and pepper. Process to combine. Add the hemp seeds and olive oil last, processing until just combined so that the texture still remains. Indulge joyfully.

Pure Pleasures

Baba Ganoush

My brother Justin is an amazingly talented chef. We always played around in the kitchen when we were kids, mixing up the weirdest foods—like liquid smoke, cottage cheese, garlic and chili powder on crackers. I can still taste that. Since then, he has professionally trained and began his career. We actually passed this recipe back and forth, from Massachusetts to Florida, as we both wanted to come up with a raw version of our favorite Lebanese dip. The chipotle in the eggplant marinade offers a mild, smoky flavor to compensate for the tradition of grilled eggplant. The rest of the ingredients are simply classic.

Makes 2 cups

Marinated Eggplant

4 cups of eggplant, peeled & thinly sliced into ¼" thick rounds (measured after slicing)
2 teaspoons Himalayan salt
¼ cup cold-pressed olive oil
2 tablespoons lemon juice
1 tablespoon raw honey
¼ cup sweet onion, diced
1 teaspoon fresh rosemary, minced
½ teaspoon ground chipotle
½ teaspoon oregano
¼ teaspoon Himalayan salt

Baba Ganoush

½ cup raw sesame tahini
¼ cup cold-pressed olive oil
2 cloves of garlic
6 tablespoons pure water
3 tablespoons lemon juice
½ teaspoon Himalayan salt

MARINATED EGGPLANT Sprinkle the eggplant with the 2 teaspoons of salt and let sit for 1-2 hours to remove the bitter juices. Rinse and pat dry. For the marinade, combine the olive oil, lemon, honey, sweet onion, rosemary, chipotle, oregano and ¼ teaspoon salt. Whisk in a large bowl. Add the eggplant to the marinade and mix well so that all sides of the eggplant are coated. Place eggplant on mesh dehydrator trays and dehydrate at 105° for 6-8 hours. When done, the eggplant should be chewy and flavorful.

BABA GANOUSH Place the tahini, olive oil, garlic, water, lemon, and salt in the food processor. Process until smooth. Add the eggplant and process again until well combined but still slightly chunky. Serve with cucumber slices, Fresh Herb & Kale Tabbouleh (*page 54*) or Tomato Basil Flatbread (*page 45*).

Pure Pleasures

Sunny Hummus

Again, raw vegan hummus is not unique, but that does not change the fact that this is my absolute favorite version and is a simple, filling staple to keep in your fridge. It is so nice and hearty, adding extra satisfaction to green salads, veggies and flax crackers.

Makes 3 cups

Ingredients

4 cloves of garlic
1½ cups raw sunflower seeds,
    soaked 4-6 hours, drained/rinsed
½ cup raw sesame tahini
½ cup lemon juice

¼ cup cold-pressed olive oil
¼ cup pure water
¾ teaspoon Himalayan salt
Olive oil, paprika and/or parsley to garnish

Preparation
Place the garlic cloves in the food processor fit with the S-blade. Process to chop. Add all of the remaining ingredients (except garnishes) and process until smooth. You may want to scrape down the sides a few times with a spatula. Scrape into a bowl, drizzle with olive oil and sprinkle with paprika and chopped parsley. Satisfy your hunger!

HERBED HEMP PARMESAN

I love to finish my live Italian dishes with a dash of hemp seed to mimic the look of grated Parmesan cheese in an instant. When you are looking for extra flavor, try this herby garnish. I love to sprinkle it on pasta, salads, lasagna and pizza as a finishing touch.

Makes 1 cup

INGREDIENTS
1 small clove of garlic
¼ teaspoon miso
1 cup hemp seeds
1 teaspoon Italian herbs
½ teaspoon Himalayan salt

PREPARATION Place the garlic and miso in the food processor fit with the S-blade. Process to finely chop the garlic and distribute the miso. Add all other ingredients and pulse a few times to combine. Store in the refrigerator for up to 2 weeks.

Vanilla Nut Butter

I love to buy pre-made raw nut butters, but they can be quite pricey. I whipped this up one day when I was really craving peanut butter. The combination of cashews and sesame oil had me fooled. Adam loves this on bananas, sprinkled with raw cacao nibs.

Makes 1½ cups

Ingredients

2 cups raw cashews
¼ cup cold-pressed sesame oil
2 tablespoons raw honey
1 vanilla bean
¼ teaspoon Himalayan salt

Preparation

Blend all ingredients in a high-speed blender until smooth. Use the tamper to keep things moving and prevent heating. Store in the refrigerator. Use as you would peanut butter.

CinnaVanilla Syrup

This is such a delicious dessert topping. I created it for the Rooibos Ice Cream, but also found it to be the most amazing drizzle on the Chai Spice Cheesecake. It makes a beautiful plate garnish as well.

Makes ½ cup

Ingredients
½ cup raw agave nectar
2 teaspoons cinnamon
Seeds of 1 vanilla bean
⅛ teaspoon Himalayan salt

Preparation
Whisk together all ingredients in small bowl. Store in the refrigerator to thicken the syrup. Serve with Rooibos Ice Cream (*page 109*) or Chai Spice Cheesecake (*page 120*).

NOURISH

Though I love to eat light and fresh, there are days when just a simple salad will not suffice. Especially in the colder months, I will crave savory dishes that are just a little bit richer and deeply satisfying. Some of them can even be served warm from the dehydrator for extra comfort. It brings me great pleasure to reminisce about the meals I shared with family growing up and that is where I draw a lot of my creative inspiration from. I can't help it—I'm an emotional foodie!

CILANTRO LIME CHICK-UN SALAD

When I was transitioning to raw foods, I was HUNGRY! I could not eat enough food to keep me full. That is when I started eating nut & seed pâtés, with lots of protein and healthy fat to keep me satisfied. I lived off of a version of this recipe for a very long time. I would eat huge portions on tiny green salads. Now fully immersed in this lifestyle, I put a bit on a huge green salad and savor every bite.

Makes 4 cups

CHICK-UN SALAD

1½ cups raw sunflower seeds,
　　soaked 4-6 hours, drained/rinsed
1 cup of celery, diced
3 scallions, diced
⅔ cup red pepper, diced
1 tablespoon poultry seasoning
1 teaspoon ground chipotle

CILANTRO-LIME MAYO

½ cup pure water
2 cloves of garlic
⅓ cup fresh lime juice
¾ teaspoon Himalayan salt
1½ cup raw pine nuts
¼ bunch of cilantro, chopped

CHICK-UN SALAD Grind the sunflower seeds in a food processor. Toss with remaining salad ingredients in a large bowl.

CILANTRO-LIME MAYO Blend all ingredients except for the cilantro until smooth and creamy. Fold in the cilantro by hand. Pour the mayo over the salad and mix well. Serve over a large green salad, dressed lightly, with lime juice and olive oil.

Pure Pleasures

SPINACH & FETA PIZZA

My mom often made a pizza with spinach, feta cheese, onions and black olives that the whole family went crazy for. When Justin got into the kitchen, he added lots of thyme and sesame seeds for even more Mediterranean authenticity. My version blends the two, but kicks it into the raw food world with all the flavor of the original. This is a recipe where a dehydrator is pretty necessary to get the full effect. If it is not possible, skip the crust, mix up the spinach and feta topping and wrap in lettuce or spread on store bought flax crackers. The depth of flavor will still be present, but the texture will of course be different.

Makes 2 dozen mini pizzas

PIZZA CRUST
1½ cups raw sunflower seeds,
    soaked 4-6 hours, drained/rinsed
1½ cups raw walnuts, soaked 4-6 hours, drained/rinsed
2 cups celery, chopped (approximately 4 stalks)
2 cups apple, chopped (approximately 2 medium apples)
2 cloves of garlic
2 teaspoons rosemary
2 teaspoons thyme
2 teaspoons oregano
¾ teaspoon Himalayan salt
⅔ cups cold-pressed olive oil
1 cup pure water
1½ cups ground flax seeds

GARNISH
Raw sesame seeds
Fresh or dried thyme
Sun dried black olives

FETA
1½ cups raw macadamia nuts,
    soaked 4-6 hours, drained/rinsed
¼ cup lemon juice
¼ cup pure water
¼ cup cold-pressed olive oil
¾ teaspoon Himalayan salt
½ teaspoon miso
2 teaspoons fresh thyme leaves
1 tablespoon oregano

MEDITERRANEAN SPINACH
¼ cup cold-pressed olive oil
¼ cup sweet onion, diced
2 cloves of garlic, minced
1½ tablespoons raw sesame seeds
1 tablespoon dried thyme
⅛ teaspoon Himalayan salt
2½ cups chopped spinach

PIZZA CRUST Separately pulse the sunflower seeds, walnuts, celery, apples, and garlic in a food processor until finely chopped. Pour all of the chopped ingredients into a large bowl and mix well. Combine the dried herbs in a pestle and mortar to release the flavors. Add the herbs, salt, olive oil and water to the bowl and mix again. Lastly, add the ground flax seeds and mix very well to assure there are no lumps. Prepare your dehydrator trays with nonstick sheets. Scoop ¼ cup of batter per crust onto the sheets. Spread into individual circles that are approximately 5" in diameter. Place in the dehydrator at 145° for 90 minutes. Flip the crusts over and remove the nonstick sheets. Turn the temperature to 105° and dehydrate for another 16-18 hours.

FETA Place the macadamia nuts in the food processor and process to finely chop. With the blade running, add the lemon and water and continue to process until smooth. Add the olive oil, salt and miso and process once again. Lastly, add your herbs and pulse until just combined.

Pure Pleasures

MEDITERRANEAN SPINACH Mix the olive oil, onion, garlic, sesame seeds, thyme and salt in a medium bowl. Allow to marinate for 10 minutes. Add the spinach and toss well to coat. Fold in the feta and mix very well.

ASSEMBLY Begin with your fully dehydrated crusts. Top each crust with 2 tablespoons of the spinach and feta mixture. Sprinkle with additional sesame seeds and thyme. Top with slices of sun dried olives. Return to the dehydrator for an additional 2 hours. Serve warm.

Chipotle Eggplant & Avocado Wraps
with Cilantro-lime Mayo

••

These are so, so, so, good… it is impossible to do them justice in words. Just make them! Dehydrating the eggplant is essential; there is just no way around it. These wraps are completely reminiscent of a BLT and are really brought to life with the creamy avocado and tangy lime mayo. When my brother Ian visited me on a summer trip, this was by far his favorite of my dishes. That says a lot to me coming from a teenager with a traditional diet. To Ian!

The Chipotle Eggplant sauce uses mesquite powder—a sweet, almost smoky powder made from the pods of a desert bush. For this recipe, get your hands on some from my suppliers listed in the back.

Serves 5

Chipotle Eggplant
½ lb eggplant
1 – 4 oz tomato (½ cup blended tomato puree)
2 tablespoons raw honey
2 tablespoons mesquite powder
2 teaspoons onion powder
1 clove of garlic
1 teaspoon ground chipotle
1 teaspoon paprika
½ teaspoon Himalayan salt
¼ cup cold-pressed olive oil

Cilantro Lime Mayo
¼ cup pure water
1 clove of garlic
¼ cup fresh lime juice
¼ teaspoon Himalayan salt
¾ cup raw pine nuts
¼ cup chopped cilantro leaves

Wraps
10 leaves of Butter lettuce
3 avocados
2 medium tomatoes

Chipotle Eggplant Slice the eggplant on a mandoline into long, thin strips. Sprinkle with salt and let sit for 1-2 hours to draw out the bitter juices. Rinse and pat dry. Cut into 1" wide strips and place in a large bowl. Blend the tomato on its own to make sure you have ½ cup of purée. Add all other ingredients and blend well. Pour this sauce over the eggplant strips and mix well so that all of the eggplant is covered. Spread the eggplant on mesh dehydrator trays in one layer. Make sure they are not covered in too much sauce or they will not become crisp. Dehydrate at 105° for 4 hours. Flip over. Dehydrate for an additional 10-12 hours. They may be chewy once done, but when placed in the refrigerator, they will become crisp.

Cilantro Lime Mayo Blend all ingredients except for the cilantro in a high-speed blender. Pour into a bowl and fold in the cilantro by hand. Chill.

Wraps For each wrap, begin with a lettuce leaf and pour on 1 tablespoon of Cilantro Lime Mayo. Top with ¼ of an avocado, diced. Add 2 teaspoons diced tomato. Top with 8 strips of Chipotle Eggplant and garnish with additional chopped cilantro if desired.

Pure Pleasures

ITALIAN SAUSAGE PATTIES
WITH RAINBOW VEGGIES AND HANDMADE MUSTARD

This is like an elegant, raw vegan version of a ball park sausage with peppers, onions and mustard. My dad is great on the grill and whenever he was serving up sausage, I loved to cover it in mustard. Be sure to make your mustard a few days in advance to let the flavors mellow. You can certainly skip the dehydrating if necessary. The drying time just adds a bit more authenticity to the texture.

Serves 6

SAUSAGE PATTIES
2 small cloves of garlic
¾ cup sun dried tomatoes, soaked 4-6 hours in pure water and chopped small (measure after chopping)
2 teaspoons oregano
2 teaspoons fennel seeds
1 teaspoon basil
¾ teaspoon fresh rosemary, finely chopped
½-1 teaspoon Himalayan salt
¼ teaspoon crushed chili pepper
3 cups raw pecans, soaked 4-6 hours, drained/rinsed and dehydrated 12-24 hours
6 tablespoons cold-pressed olive oil

RAINBOW VEGGIES
1½ cups multi colored mini bell peppers, sliced thinly on a mandoline
1 packed cup spinach, thinly shredded
½ cup red onion, sliced thinly on a mandoline
1 clove of garlic, minced
1 teaspoon oregano
1 teaspoon fresh rosemary
1 teaspoon fresh thyme
3 tablespoons cold-pressed olive oil
1½ tablespoons lemon juice
¼ teaspoon Himalayan salt

HANDMADE MUSTARD
See recipe on page 66

SAUSAGE PATTIES Chop the garlic in the food processor and scrape down the sides. Add the sun dried tomatoes and all of the herbs and spices. Process well. Add the nuts and olive oil and process until fairly smooth and well combined, making sure all the nuts are finely ground. Scoop out 2 tablespoons and shape into ½" thick, round patties. Place on mesh dehydrator trays and dehydrate at 110° for 6-8 hours.

RAINBOW VEGGIES Toss all ingredients in a medium bowl. Let sit 30 minutes to marinate.

Pleasures

HANDMADE MUSTARD See recipe on page 66.

ASSEMBLY Per serving, place three patties on a plate in a triangular shape. Top with ¼ cup of rainbow veggies, placed in the center of the triangle. Serve with a spoonful of mustard on the side for dipping.

GARDEN HERB ROLL-UPS

Talk about fresh taste—it just does not get greener than this! With live food, you can get creative with wrapping and rolling using big green collard leaves and your filling of choice. I love to make nut and seed pâtés as I find them extremely nourishing and satisfying. This wrap is full of flavor with a fresh herb and pumpkin seed pâté and marinated veggies. Ditch the tortillas, grab some collards, and have some fun in the kitchen!

Serves 6

PUMPKIN SEED PÂTÉ
2 cloves of garlic
½ cup raw Brazil nuts
½ cup lemon juice
1½ cups raw pumpkin seeds,
    soaked 4-6 hours, drained/rinsed
¼ cup cold-pressed olive oil
¾ teaspoon Himalayan salt
¼ cup parsley
¼ cup basil
¼ cup dill

MARINATED VEGGIES
2 cups baby spinach
1½ cups shredded carrots
¼ cup sweet onion, very thinly sliced
2 tablespoons cold-pressed olive oil
2 teaspoons lemon juice
¼ teaspoon Himalayan salt
Black pepper to taste

ASSEMBLY
6 large collard leaves
3 Roma tomatoes, thinly sliced

PUMPKIN SEED PÂTÉ Place the garlic in your food processor fit with the S-blade. Process to chop. Add the Brazil nuts and process until they are finely chopped. With the blade running, add the lemon juice until the mixture is creamy. Add the pumpkin seeds, olive oil and salt to the processor and continue to purée. Lastly, add the parsley, basil and dill and pulse to finely chop the herbs. Scrape into a bowl.

MARINATED VEGGIES Toss all ingredients in a large bowl and mix well to combine all of the flavors.

ASSEMBLY Lay a collard green on your cutting board with the darker side on the board. Chop off the stem and trim off any very thick portions of the remaining center stem. Place 6 tablespoons of the pâté on the collard leaf and spread out a bit, but leave plenty of room for wrapping up the leaf. Top with a few slices of tomato. Cover with ½ cup of the marinated veggies. Roll up just like a burrito, folding up the top and bottom first and then rolling in the sides. Cut each wrap in half to serve. Enjoy!

Pure Pleasures

Spinach Quesadillas
with Smoky Cilantro Cheese
••

This is another one of those recipes where you will be so happy that you have a dehydrator. The perfectly flexible tortilla, wrapped around smoky chipotle cheese, tangy marinated spinach and creamy avocado make for an almost unbelievable raw dish. Please, someone, make this and share with me, pretty please!

Serves 8

Tortillas
1 cup chopped tomato
1 cup chopped carrots
¾ cup chopped red pepper
¼ cup pure water
2 tablespoons onion
2 cloves of garlic
1 teaspoon cumin
1 teaspoon chili powder
¾ teaspoon Himalayan salt
½ cup cold-pressed olive oil
¾ cup ground flax seeds

Smoky Cilantro Cheese
¾ cup chopped orange bell pepper
½ cup cold-pressed olive oil
⅓ cup lemon juice
6 tablespoons pure water
1 teaspoon Himalayan salt
¾ teaspoon miso
2 teaspoons ground chipotle
3 cups raw macadamia nuts
   soaked 4-6 hours, drained/rinsed
½ cup cilantro leaves, chopped
½ cup scallions, chopped

Wilted Spinach
7 cups spinach, cut into thin ribbons
2 tablespoons lime juice
2 tablespoons cold-pressed olive oil
2 cloves of garlic, minced
¼ cup chopped cilantro
¼ teaspoon Himalayan salt

Assembly
2 avocados

TORTILLAS Place the tomato, carrot, red pepper, water, onion, garlic, cumin, chili and salt in a blender and blend until smooth. Add the olive oil and blend to combine. Pour into a bowl and whisk in the flax seeds until smooth and all lumps are gone. Divide the batter over two dehydrator trays lined with nonstick sheets. Spread out evenly to the edges. Dehydrate at 105° for 4-6 hours. Flip over and remove the nonstick sheets. Dehydrate for an additional 6-8 hours until dry in the centers, but still flexible.

SMOKY CILANTRO CHEESE Process the bell pepper, olive oil, lemon, water, salt, miso and chipotle until well combined. Add in the macadamia nuts and process until smooth. Pour into a bowl and mix in the cilantro and scallions by hand.

WILTED SPINACH Toss all ingredients in a bowl and mix well with your hands to soften and wilt the spinach.

Pure Pleasures

ASSEMBLY Divide the Smoky Cilantro Cheese and Wilted Spinach in two equal portions. Spread the cheese over the full square of each tortilla evenly. Top each cheese layer with spinach. Dehydrate for 2 hours at 105° to warm. Slice the 2 avocados and lay out evenly over the spinach on half of each quesadilla. Using a spatula for support, fold the tortilla in half over the avocado layer. Move to a cutting board and cut into 2 squares. Cut each square into triangles. Serve with Sunny Sour Cream and Salsa Fresca from the Seven Layer Taco Dip recipe (*page 36*).

GREEK KALE STUFFED TOMATOES
WITH HERBED FETA

This recipe combines two of my all time favorite things—marinated kale and macadamia based cheese. Stuffing it all inside a ripe, juicy tomato makes a beautiful presentation. This is a fabulous dish to serve to dinner guests as an impressive introduction to live food.

Serves 5

GREEK KALE
9 cups shredded kale
½ teaspoon Himalayan salt
¼ cup cold-pressed olive oil
¼ cup lemon juice
2 cloves of garlic, minced
⅓ cup raw pumpkin seeds
¾ cup red bell pepper, diced
¼ cup onion, diced
3 tablespoons chopped dill
⅛ teaspoon black pepper

HERBED FETA
1½ cups raw macadamia nuts,
    soaked 4-6 hours, drained/rinsed
¼ cup lemon juice
¼ cup pure water
¼ cup cold-pressed olive oil
¾ teaspoons Himalayan salt
½ teaspoons miso
2 teaspoons fresh thyme leaves
1 tablespoon oregano

ASSEMBLY
10 small tomatoes
10 sun dried black olives, halved
Olive oil and additional thyme for garnishing

GREEK KALE To shred your kale, stack a few leaves at a time, and cut into very thin ribbons. Place in a large bowl and sprinkle with the salt. Using your hands, massage the salt into the kale, squeezing and tossing until the kale begins to wilt. Add your olive oil, lemon and garlic and continue to massage, further softening the kale. Once the kale is nice and soft and very dark green in color, you are ready to add the remaining ingredients. Toss all ingredients very well and set aside.

HERBED FETA Place the macadamia nuts in the food processor and process to finely chop. With the blade running, add the lemon juice and water and continue to process until smooth. Add the olive oil, salt and miso and process once again. Lastly, add your herbs and pulse until just combined.

ASSEMBLY Cut each tomato in half and use a spoon to scoop out the seeds. Fill each tomato half with ¼ cup of Greek Kale. Top with a heaping tablespoon of Herbed Feta. Place four halves on a plate for each serving. Drizzle with olive oil and top each with an olive and a sprig of thyme.

Pure Pleasures

SAAG PANEER

Mmmm…Indian food—totally a favorite in my family. I love the strong spices and cooling accompaniments for a balanced plate. Here I have created a nicely spiced, creamed spinach with chunks of dehydrated macadamia "paneer" for a really special dish. It is very reminiscent of the traditional Saag Paneer I used to enjoy at my favorite Indian restaurant. This is rich and deeply satisfying; a beautiful dish to serve in the wintertime while it is still warm from the dehydrator. Even if you don't have a dehydrator, just serve up the creamed spinach with dollops of macadamia paneer and it will still be sure to nourish.

Serves 4

SAAG

1¼ cups raw cashews, soaked 2 hours, drained/rinsed
½ cup lemon juice
1 teaspoon Himalayan salt
1 lb baby spinach
2 tablespoons cold-pressed olive oil
3 cloves of garlic, minced
½ teaspoon ginger, grated
¾ cup fresh cilantro, chopped
½ cup onion, diced
½ teaspoon chili powder
½ teaspoon cumin
½ teaspoon garam masala
½ teaspoon turmeric
¼ teaspoon coriander

MACADAMIA PANEER

1½ cups raw macadamia nuts, soaked 4-6 hours, drained/rinsed
¼ cup lemon juice
¼ cup pure water
¼ cup cold-pressed olive oil
¾ teaspoons Himalayan salt
½ teaspoon miso

SAAG In a high-speed blender, combine the cashews, lemon juice and salt. Blend until smooth. Scrape into a large bowl. Place a few handfuls of the spinach in a food processor fit with the S-blade. Pulse to roughly chop. Scrape into the bowl with the cashew cream. Repeat until you have chopped all of the spinach. Add the olive oil, garlic, ginger, cilantro, onion, chili, cumin, garam masala, turmeric and coriander to the bowl. Mix very well. If desired, spread onto two dehydrator sheets lined with nonstick sheets and dehydrate at 105° for 1-2 hours until warm.

Pure Pleasures

MACADAMIA PANEER Place the macadamia nuts in a food processor fit with the S-blade. Pulse to chop. Add the lemon, water, olive oil, salt and miso to the food processor. Process until smooth. Prepare your dehydrator sheets with nonstick sheets. Spread the mixture into ½" thick by 1" wide squares. Dehydrate at 105° for 2 hours. Flip them over and remove the nonstick sheet. Continue to dehydrate for another 2 hours until the outside edges are firm and dry. The inside will remain creamy.

SERVING Divide the Saag among 4 plates. Divide the Macadamia Paneer and place on top of the Saag. Mix each portion gently. Enjoy the pleasures of being so deeply nourished.

PEA-NAUGHTY VEGGIES

I always loved peanut butter in anything—desserts, on noodles, and covering Asian veggies. This is a peanut inspired Asian sauce, though made from a combination of Brazil nuts and sesame oil. It is really rich, indulgent and almost naughty, but packed full of nutrition. This is another recipe where dehydration is purely optional. Do so if you want to soften and warm the veggies a bit, especially during the colder months.

Serves 6

VEGGIES
1 cup broccoli, cut very thin
1 cup bell pepper, sliced very thin
¾ cup carrots, cut into thin rounds
1½ cups snow peas
½ head cabbage, shredded very thin
2½ cups bok choy, shredded
½ cup chopped scallions
⅓ cup cilantro, chopped
⅓ cup raw sesame seeds

PEA-NAUGHTY SAUCE
2 cups raw Brazil nuts
½ cup + 2 tablespoons cold-pressed sesame oil
¼ cup coconut aminos
3 cloves of garlic
1¼ teaspoon grated ginger
1 teaspoon umeboshi vinegar
2 tablespoons raw honey
¼ teaspoon cayenne pepper

VEGGIES Toss all of the veggies in a large bowl.

PEA-NAUGHTY SAUCE Combine all of the ingredients in a blender until smooth. Pour over the veggies and toss very well to coat. Serve immediately or dehydrate for 1-2 hours at 105° to warm.

Pure Pleasures

FETTUCCINE WITH FRESH TOMATO & HERB SAUCE

For all the seasoned raw foodies in the house, you know zucchini pasta is a super popular dish. I never really got into the spiralized noodles, though. They are always a little too firm and bitter for me to think I am eating pasta. When I created this dish, I was thrilled! The thinness of the noodles that a simple vegetable peeler will create allows them to be quickly and deeply flavored with the spicy garlic oil. Topped with a super fresh tomato and herb sauce, this should be pleasing to all!

Serves 2

FETTUCCINE
3 tablespoons cold-pressed olive oil
1 clove of garlic, minced
¼ teaspoon crushed chili pepper
¼ teaspoon Himalayan salt
3 medium zucchini

FRESH TOMATO & HERB SAUCE
3 Roma tomatoes, diced
1 clove of garlic, minced
½ teaspoon Himalayan salt
1 tablespoon cold-pressed olive oil
¼ cup roughly chopped fresh basil
3 tablespoons finely chopped fresh parsley
1½ teaspoon finely chopped fresh oregano
1 small scallion, finely chopped
¼ cup hemp seeds

FETTUCCINE In a large bowl, whisk together the olive oil, garlic, chili and salt. Set aside. Wash and peel your zucchini. Using the peeler, create long strips of zucchini fettuccine about ¼"-½" wide. Keep rotating the zucchini so that you are peeling all edges rather than continuously peeling in the same spot. When you get to the center of the zucchini and it becomes quite seedy, stop peeling and set aside. Save for later and use in a green juice, salad or blended soup. Continue peeling the remaining zucchini according to this method. Toss all of your fettuccine with the garlic oil. Set aside.

FRESH TOMATO & HERB SAUCE In a large bowl, toss all ingredients together and mix well.

ASSEMBLY Strain the pasta as it will have released a lot of liquid. Divide over two plates. Top each serving of pasta with half of the Fresh Tomato & Herb Sauce. Alternately, you can toss everything together in one big bowl and serve that way. Indulge in pure pleasure!

Pure Pleasures

HERBED TOMATO FANS

I absolutely love the flavors of deep, dark greens, fresh herbs and tart lemon playing together. Here, my herb salad is paired with a luscious garlic-walnut spread and ripe, juicy tomatoes. So yummy, super easy, and makes a gorgeous presentation. Get ready to impress!

Serves 6

GARLIC WALNUT SPREAD
2 cloves of garlic
2 cups raw walnuts, soaked 4-6 hours, drained/rinsed
¼ cup pure water
¼ cup lemon juice
¼ cup cold-pressed olive oil
¾ teaspoon Himalayan salt

HERB SALAD
2½ cups spinach
½ cup parsley
½ cup dill
2 tablespoons lemon juice
2 tablespoons cold-pressed olive oil
1 clove of garlic, minced
½ teaspoon Himalayan salt
⅛ teaspoon freshly ground black pepper

ASSEMBLY
12 Roma tomatoes
Additional Baby Spinach or mixed greens for serving

GARLIC WALNUT SPREAD Process the garlic in your food processor fit with the S-blade. Add the walnuts and process again until finely ground. Add the water, lemon, olive oil and salt and process until smooth. Scrape into a bowl and set aside.

HERB SALAD Place the spinach, parsley and dill in the clean food processor and pulse until finely chopped. Scrape into a bowl and toss with the lemon, olive oil, garlic, salt and pepper.

ASSEMBLY Cut each tomato into 7 slices, each equal in thickness. Starting with the bottom slice of each tomato, top every other slice with 1 tablespoon of walnut spread until you have covered 4 slices. Cover the remaining 3 slices with 1 tablespoon of herb salad. For each serving, prepare 2 tomatoes. Lay out in a pretty fan pattern on a bed of spinach or baby greens.

Pure Pleasures

SWEET TREATS

I find the most foodie pleasure in creating and indulging in desserts. Live food has reawakened my sweet tooth. I enjoy a bit of sweetness everyday. I love living guilt-free, knowing that even my desserts are full of nutrition. They always bring the most compliments and are the easiest way to introduce a newbie to live food.

CHOCOLATE CHERRY TRUFFLES

Cherries are one of my favorite summer fruits. I cannot stop eating them! Chocolate and cherries are a classic combination, but at first glance, there is no way to tell there is a sweet, fresh cherry wrapped up inside these little bites. I love surprises! The truffle base is so simple, you can play around with your favorite fruits, nuts and spices to create your own masterpiece. Be creative and have fun!

Makes one dozen

INGREDIENTS

¾ cup raw cacao powder
Seeds of 1 vanilla bean
Pinch of Himalayan salt
½ cup pitted Medjool dates

¼ cup raw honey
1 tablespoon cold-pressed coconut oil
12 pitted cherries
2 tablespoons raw cacao powder for dusting

PREPARATION Place the ¾ cup of cacao powder, vanilla bean and salt in a food processor. Pulse gently to combine. Add the dates, honey and coconut oil and process again until sticky and smooth. To make each truffle, roll about one tablespoon of chocolate into a 1" ball with your hands. Flatten into a circle and wrap around the cherry. Roll again to make a smooth, round ball. Place the 2 tablespoons of cacao powder on a plate. Roll each cherry filled truffle in the cacao powder and give it one last roll with your hands for an even coating. Set in the refrigerator for one hour to firm. Consume within 2 days since you're using fresh cherries, or freeze for longer storage.

Pure Pleasures

Jungle Balls

This recipe is a big shout out to my girl Addie! She always made a treat just like this for me and all of her other vegan friends. My hubby Adam went absolutely crazy for them. So much so, that he would actually get in the kitchen and make them so he could eat a whole batch on his own. We were really missing them, as the original contains a few ingredients that we do not use anymore. A little kitchen magic and voilà—Jungle Balls are here to stay, and yes, they are Adam approved.

Makes 16 cookies

Jungle Balls
2 cups raw Brazil nuts
¼ cup cold-pressed sesame oil
¼ teaspoon Himalayan salt
⅓ cup cold-pressed coconut oil
⅓ cup raw honey
Seeds of 1 vanilla bean
1⅔ cups raw cashews

Chocolate Stripes
¼ cup cold-pressed coconut oil
3 tablespoons raw agave nectar
½ cup raw cacao powder
Pinch of Himalayan salt

JUNGLE BALLS Place the Brazil nuts, sesame oil and salt in a high-speed blender. Slowly blend from low to high until creamy. Scrape into a large bowl. Add the coconut oil, honey and vanilla bean seeds and mix well. In a food processor, process the cashews into a flour-like texture. Pour into the bowl and mix until well combined. Place in the refrigerator to firm for 1-2 hours. Remove from the refrigerator. Roll into 1½" balls and place on a cookie sheet lined with wax paper. Place in the freezer to set completely for 2 hours.

CHOCOLATE STRIPES In a medium sized bowl, whisk together the coconut oil and agave. Slowly add cacao powder and salt and whisk until very smooth. Pour into a piping bag or a sandwich bag with a small corner cut off. Decorate frozen cookies with lovely chocolate stripes. Store in the freezer. Thaw 10 minutes prior to serving. Share the yummies with friends!

Pure Pleasures

SWEETIE SUSHI

I have always loved the presentation of sushi; it is a complete work of art. Unfortunately, I have a total aversion to sea veggies, which is a shame because they are so mineral rich and healthy. I'm workin' on it! For my palate, a dessert sushi is the perfect solution. This is great for kids whose palates may not be ready for nori and for adults who just want to have some more fun with food.

Makes 48 pieces

SUSHI WRAPS
3 bananas
1 - 10 oz bag frozen blueberries, thawed
2 tablespoons raw honey
2 tablespoons cold-pressed coconut oil

STICKY RICE
1 cup raw macadamia nuts
⅛ teaspoon Himalayan salt
3 cups shredded coconut
2 tablespoons raw honey
½ teaspoon vanilla extract

FRUIT FILLING
2 avocados
½ papaya
1 mango
¼ pineapple

CITRUS DIPPING SAUCE
1 cup orange juice
2 tablespoons raw honey
1½ tablespoons lime juice
1 tablespoon coconut aminos
½ teaspoon freshly grated ginger

SUSHI WRAPS Blend the bananas, blueberries and honey until smooth. Making sure the mixture is warm enough to melt the coconut oil, add the oil and blend until just combined. Divide the puree in half and pour onto 2 dehydrator trays lined with nonstick sheets. Spread out evenly to the edges. Dehydrate at 105° for 8 hours. Flip over and remove the nonstick sheets. Dehydrate for an additional 4-6 hours until dry all the way through. Once done, cut each sheet into 4 equal squares to resemble nori sheets. Store at room temperature.

STICKY RICE Place the macadamia nuts and salt in a food processor. Process until the nuts are finely chopped and sticky. Add the coconut and process again. Add the honey and vanilla and pulse until all ingredients are well combined and sticky.

FRUIT FILLING Cut all of the fruits into strips about ½" thick and 4" long.

Pure Pleasure

CITRUS DIPPING SAUCE Blend all ingredients until well combined.

ASSEMBLY Begin with a Sushi Wrap. Top with approximately ⅓ cup of your sticky rice. Press down to flatten so that it reaches the edges from left to right, but leave about 2" of open space on both the top and the bottom of the wrap for rolling. Top the rice with strips of fruit so that you have one row of each variety running from left to right in the center of your rice. Roll the wrap away from you, keeping everything tight and secure. Use a little honey to keep the wrap closed at the end. Cut each sushi roll into 6 equal pieces using a very sharp knife. Serve with dipping sauce on the side. Sprinkle with black sesame seed if desired. Have fun playing with your food!

TRUE LOVE CHOCOLATE HAZELNUT HEARTS

In the food world, nothing speaks the language of love like chocolate. These are a great treat for Valentine's Day or anniversaries. I adore a holiday that celebrates love. For my sweetie, I created these raw & organic chocolate hearts. Deep, dark cacao caresses a sweet hazelnut filling for a rich, dreamy indulgence. Enjoying the single life right now? Share the love with friends, family & yourself. Everyone deserves chocolate love.

Servings will vary depending on your mold, but you will have plenty to share.

CHOCOLATE
½ cup cold-pressed coconut oil
6 tablespoons raw agave nectar
Seeds of ½ vanilla bean
1 cup raw cacao powder

HAZELNUT FILLING
¾ cup raw hazelnuts
2 tablespoons raw agave nectar
2 teaspoons cold-pressed coconut oil
Seeds of ½ vanilla bean
Pinch of Himalayan salt

CHOCOLATE Pour the coconut oil into a medium sized bowl. Add the agave and vanilla. Whisk to combine. Slowly add your cacao powder while whisking to ensure there are no lumps. Whisk until you have a very smooth, shiny chocolate.

HAZELNUT FILLING Place the hazelnuts in a food processor. Process into a fine powder. Remove 2 tablespoons to be used for decoration later. Add the agave, coconut oil, vanilla and salt to your food processor. Process again until the mixture is smooth and sticks together.

ASSEMBLY Select a mold. I like silicone for its easy release. I use heart shaped cupcake molds. For a cupcake sized mold, fill the bottom of each with 1 tablespoon of chocolate. Spread up the sides so that the chocolate covers ½" in height on the sides and is about ¼" deep on the bottom. Continue until ⅔ of the chocolate has been used. Place in the refrigerator for 1 hour until completely firm. Remove from the refrigerator. For each chocolate, place 2 teaspoons of the Hazelnut Filling in the center of the heart. Press down to flatten, but leave ¼" of empty space all the way around the edges to cover in chocolate. Pour ½ tablespoon of chocolate over the hazelnut filling, making sure to fill the empty edge. Sprinkle the tops with your reserved hazelnuts for decoration. Return to the refrigerator for another 1-2 hours to set completely. Remove from the refrigerator and pop out of the molds. Let stand at room temperature for 10 minutes before serving.

Alternately, if you don't have silicone molds available: divide your chocolate in two equal portions. Spread half of the chocolate into an 8" square baking dish lined with wax paper for easy removal. Refrigerate to set as above. Cover with your hazelnut mixture and press downs evenly. Cover with remaining chocolate and refrigerate to set completely. Remove from the dish and place on a cutting board. Remove the wax and cut into squares, triangles, or use a cookie cutter for some fun shapes.

PISTACHIO CRUSTED FRUITS

This is a simple but elegant dessert or sweet appetizer. In the summer, I love to showcase ripe, juicy fruits and gently complement them with other flavors and textures. I love how the bright green pistachios contrast against the red fruits, and of course, they taste fabulous!

Serves 4

INGREDIENTS
½ lb cherries
½ lb strawberries
3 tablespoons raw agave nectar
¼ cup pistachios
Pinch of Himalayan salt

PREPARATION Wash and dry your fruits. Pour the agave into a small bowl. Chop the pistachios in a food processor until finely ground. Pour into another small bowl and mix with the salt. Dip the fruit in to the agave and let the excess drip off. Roll the agave coated fruit in the pistachios and place on a platter. Repeat until all of your fruit is covered.

Pure Pleasures

MINT CHIP MACAROONS

I love sweets that are so quick and easy that you can throw them together at the same time you are making dinner and have a sweet bite ready when you are. These are so fresh tasting when you use high quality organic peppermint extract and the crunchy cacao nibs complement them perfectly.

Makes two dozen

INGREDIENTS

½ cup cold-pressed coconut oil
½ cup raw honey **or** raw agave nectar
¾ teaspoon peppermint extract

Pinch of Himalayan salt
3 tablespoons raw cacao nibs
2½ cups finely shredded coconut

PREPARATION Mix the coconut oil, honey, peppermint, salt and cacao nibs in a large bowl. Pour the coconut into the same bowl and mix well to combine all ingredients. Use a small scoop to create bite sized balls, placing them on a cookie sheet or platter. When time is of the essence, you can spread the entire mixture into a 9" square baking dish. With either method, place the macaroons in the freezer for 1-2 hours to set. Thaw 15 minutes before serving. If you opted for the square dish, cut into desired shapes after thawing.

ROOIBOS ICE CREAM

I love rooibos tea for its high levels of antioxidants, lack of caffeine and lovely flavor. Of course, I love ice cream too and this is a smashing combination with creamy cashews and vanilla beans. If you love green tea ice cream, give this one a try. Adding a drizzle of CinnaVanilla Syrup sends this over the top.

Makes one quart

INGREDIENTS

2½ cups strong rooibos tea, cooled
2 cups raw cashews, soaked 2 hours, drained/rinsed
2 vanilla beans

½ cup raw honey
Pinch of Himalayan salt
1 cup cold-pressed coconut oil

PREPARATION Blend all ingredients except coconut oil in a high-speed blender until very smooth. Add the coconut oil and blend until well combined. Chill in the refrigerator until cold. Pour into an ice cream maker and process according to the manufacturer's instructions. If you do not have an ice cream maker, place in a large bowl. Put the bowl in the freezer and stir every half hour until thoroughly chilled and very creamy. Serve with CinnaVanilla Syrup (*page 75*).

PRETTY PARFAIT

I love fruit based desserts in the summer, full of natural, juicy sweetness! This is a quick and easy parfait that you can make with any fresh, ripe fruit that you have on hand. I love strawberries and kiwis for a bright & colorful combination. Layered with vanilla bean cream and sweet, crunchy pecans, this combination of flavors and textures is so pleasurable!

Serves 4

VANILLA BEAN CREAM
¾ cup raw macadamia nuts,
   soaked 2-4 hours, drained/rinsed
3 oz pure water
2 tablespoons raw honey
Seeds of 1 vanilla bean
¼ cup cold-pressed coconut oil

PECAN CRUNCHIES
1 cup raw pecans, soaked 4-6 hours, drained/rinsed
   and dehydrated 12-24 hours
2 tablespoons raw honey
½ teaspoon cinnamon
Pinch of Himalayan salt
¼ cup shredded coconut

FRESH FRUIT
2 cups sliced strawberries
4 kiwis, peeled, cut in half and sliced

VANILLA BEAN CREAM Place the macadamia nuts, water, honey and vanilla bean in a high-speed blender. Blend on high until smooth. With the blender running, add the coconut oil last and blend until just combined.

PECAN CRUNCHIES Roughly chop the pecans either by hand or in a food processor. Keep them chunky. Mix the honey, cinnamon and salt in a medium bowl. Add the pecans to the honey mixture and stir well to coat. Sprinkle with coconut and mix well.

ASSEMBLY For each parfait, layer as follows:

1. ¼ cup strawberries
2. ½ of a kiwi
3. 2 tablespoons Vanilla Bean Cream
4. ¼ cup Pecan Crunchies
5. ¼ cup strawberries
6. ½ of a kiwi
7. 2 tablespoons Vanilla Bean Cream
8. Garnish with any extra fruit
9. 2 tablespoons Pecan Crunchies

Enjoy with pleasure!

Pure Pleasures

MOJITO TART

The fusion of mint and lime is so pleasing—and even more so in a rich, creamy, dreamy tart. You will love this! It is a fabulous, refreshing, summertime sweet and there will be plenty to share with friends & family.

Makes one 11" tart

CRUST
1 cup raw hazelnuts
¼ cup dates
2 tablespoons cold-pressed coconut oil
Pinch of Himalayan salt

MOJITO CREAM
2 cups raw cashews, soaked 2 hours, drained/rinsed
1 avocado
1 cup lime juice
1 cup raw agave nectar
Zest of one lime
¾ cup cold-pressed coconut oil
½ cup mint leaves

CRUST Place the hazelnuts in a food processor and process until finely ground. Add all remaining ingredients to the food processor and process again until everything begins to stick together. Scrape into an 11" tart mold and press into the bottom only. Place in the freezer to set.

MOJITO CREAM Place all ingredients except for the coconut oil and mint in a high-speed blender. Blend from low to high until very smooth. Add the coconut oil and blend again until well combined. Lastly, add the mint and blend gently until the cream is speckled with fine bits of mint. Pour onto the crust and smooth out the top. Place back in the freezer to set completely, for 2-3 hours. Let thaw 10 minutes before serving. Yum!

Pure Pleasures

BLUEBERRY MOUSSE TART
WITH CANDIED LEMON SYRUP

This is a fun tart to serve guests—make them guess what's making the filling creamy! Avocado is a complete surprise when blended with sweet blueberries and lemon. The sweet and tart lemon syrup drizzled on the top really makes this dessert shine.

Makes one 11" tart

CRUST
1½ cups raw pecans, soaked 4-6 hours, drained/rinsed and dehydrated 12-24 hours
¼ cup pitted Medjool dates
½ teaspoon lemon zest
¼ teaspoon cinnamon
Pinch of nutmeg
Pinch of Himalayan salt

BLUEBERRY MOUSSE
3 ripe avocados
2¾ cups blueberries, fresh or thawed
6 tablespoons lemon juice
1 teaspoon lemon zest
⅔ cup raw honey
½ of a vanilla bean
Pinch of Himalayan salt
½ cup cold-pressed coconut oil

CANDIED LEMON SYRUP
¼ cup raw agave nectar
Zest of one lemon, very finely grated

CRUST Process the pecans in your food processor, fit with the S-blade, until finely ground. Add the dates, lemon zest, spices & salt and process until sticky. Press into the bottom of an 11" tart pan with a removable bottom. Place in the freezer to set while you prepare the mousse.

BLUEBERRY MOUSSE Blend all ingredients except coconut oil in a high-speed blender until smooth and creamy. Add the coconut oil last and blend until well combined. Pour the mousse over the crust. Set in the freezer for 3-4 hours until completely set in the center.

CANDIED LEMON SYRUP Whisk together the agave and lemon zest in a small bowl

TO SERVE Cut the tart while frozen and allow servings to thaw 20 minutes before serving. Drizzle Candied Lemon Syrup over slices of the tart when serving.

Pure Pleasures

CHOCOLATE MINT MOUSSE CAKE

Chocolate and mint are a match made in heaven and one of my favorite combinations. The cake here is like a fudgy brownie and the mousse is like a super tall layer of chocolate mint icing. There's so much to love in every bite.

Makes one 9" round cake

CHOCOLATE BROWNIE CAKE

4 cups raw Brazil nuts
¾ cup raw agave nectar
1 cup raw cacao powder
2 tablespoons cold-pressed coconut oil
Pinch of Himalayan salt

CHOCOLATE MINT MOUSSE

2¾ cups raw walnuts, soaked 4-6 hours, drained/rinsed
1 cup raw agave nectar
1 cup pure water
¾ cup raw cacao powder
½ cup cold-pressed coconut oil
1 vanilla bean
½ teaspoon peppermint extract

DARK CHOCOLATE GLOSS

5 tablespoons raw agave nectar
3 tablespoons cold-pressed coconut oil
½ cup raw cacao powder

CHOCOLATE BROWNIE CAKE Place the Brazil nuts in a food processor fit with the S-blade. Process until finely ground. Add the agave, cacao, coconut oil and salt and process until a sticky dough forms. Press into the bottom of a 9" spring form pan. Place in the freezer to set.

CHOCOLATE MINT MOUSSE Combine all ingredients in a high-speed blender and blend until very smooth. Pour over the Chocolate Brownie Cake. Place the entire cake in the freezer for 3-4 hours to set.

DARK CHOCOLATE GLOSS Whisk together the agave, coconut oil and cacao powder until smooth and shiny. Drizzle artistically over the entire frozen cake. Slice the cake and thaw slightly. Serve & indulge.

Pure Pleasures

CHOCOLATE BANANA CREAM TART
WITH A CHOCOLATE CHIP COOKIE CRUST

I whipped this up while traveling for my brother Ian's 17th Birthday. It totally impressed my family and no one missed traditional cake. I am always in charge of the Birthday desserts anyway, so they have definitely evolved over the years. The texture of the filling is so smooth and contrasts nicely with the crunchy crust. Share a slice with someone you love.

Makes one 11" tart

CHOCOLATE CHIP COOKIE CRUST
2 cups raw Brazil nuts
3 tablespoons raw honey
2 tablespoons cold-pressed sesame oil
Generous pinch of Himalayan salt
2 tablespoons raw cacao nibs

CHOCOLATE BANANA CREAM
7 ripe bananas
1 cup raw cacao powder
½ cup raw honey
¾ cup raw sesame tahini
½ cup cold-pressed coconut oil
1 vanilla bean
Pinch of Himalayan salt

TOPPING
1-2 bananas sliced very thin
2 tablespoons cold-pressed coconut oil
2 tablespoons raw agave nectar
¼ cup raw cacao powder

CHOCOLATE CHIP COOKIE CRUST Place the Brazil nuts in a food processor fit with the S-blade and process until finely ground. Add the honey, sesame oil and salt and pulse until evenly combined and sticky. Add the cacao nibs and pulse a few times to evenly distribute. Press into an 11" tart pan, evenly covering the bottom and sides of the pan. Place in the freezer to set while you make the filling.

CHOCOLATE BANANA CREAM Purée the bananas in a blender. You should have 4 cups of banana purée. Add the cacao powder, honey, tahini, coconut oil, vanilla bean & salt and blend well until very smooth. Pour into the tart crust and freeze to set, at least 4 hours, before topping.

TOPPING Cover the entire tart in an even, single layer of banana slices. In a small bowl, whisk together the coconut oil, agave and cacao powder. Drizzle over the bananas. Place in the refrigerator until ready to serve. Let stand at room temperature 10 minutes before serving.

Pure Pleasures

CHAI SPICE CHEESECAKE

This is definitely the favorite dessert among my friends. I love the sweet, warming spiciness—especially in the colder months and around holidays. Serve this with CinnaVanilla Syrup when you need an ultimate pleasure fix.

Makes one 9" cheesecake

CINNAMON CRUST
1 cup pecans, soaked 4-6 hours, drained/rinsed and dehydrated 12-24 hours
3 tablespoons raw honey
1 tablespoon cold-pressed coconut oil
¾ teaspoon cinnamon
¼ teaspoon nutmeg
Pinch of Himalayan salt

CHAI SPICE FILLING
3 cups raw cashews, soaked 2 hours, drained/rinsed
¾ cup pure water
¼ cup lemon juice
¾ cup raw honey
1 vanilla bean
2 teaspoons cinnamon
1 teaspoon fresh ginger, grated
¾ teaspoon cardamom
½ teaspoon nutmeg
½ teaspoon anise seed
¼ teaspoon allspice
¼ teaspoon cloves
1 cup cold-pressed coconut oil

CINNAMON CRUST Pulse the pecans in your food processor until finely ground. Add remaining ingredients and process until a sticky dough forms. Press into the bottom of a 9" round spring form pan. Place in the freezer to set.

CHAI SPICE FILLING Place all ingredients in a high-speed blender and blend until very smooth and creamy. Pour over the Cinnamon Crust and smooth out the top. Place in the freezer to set for 3-4 hours. Remove from the freezer and cut. Let thaw 10 minutes before serving. Serve with CinnaVanilla Syrup (*page 75*). Oh yeah, it is on!

Pure Pleasures

LET ME EAT CAKE!

Birthdays are a huge deal to me. Everyone deserves a special day to be celebrated. My mom always made a beautiful heart shaped, pink frosted cake to celebrate me. It's hard to let go of those things, so I decided I was going to play with raw coconut flour until I had created a cake that made it so I never had to long for Mom's cake again. The coconut flour really makes for a fluffy texture—a lot less dense than the nut based raw desserts. Here is a little collection of my favorite flavor combinations. Celebrate anything and everything with the pleasures of cake!

Pure Pleasures

LUSCIOUS LEMON LAYER CAKE

Sometimes I just way overdo the chocolate. It's good to switch things up once in a while. So, when I'm feeling like I need a break from cacao, it's time for Luscious Lemon Layer Cake! This is moist and light complemented by a rich icing…the way cake should be!

Makes one 8" four layer cake

LEMON CAKE
2½ cups peeled and chopped apples
1 cup raw honey
½ cup lemon juice
½ cup cold-pressed coconut oil
3 teaspoons lemon zest
¼ teaspoon turmeric
Pinch of Himalayan salt
3 cups raw coconut flour

LEMON COCONUT ICING
2 cups raw cashews, soaked 2 hours, drained/rinsed
¾ cup raw honey
½ cup lemon juice
½ cup coconut butter*
½ cup pure water
1½ teaspoons lemon zest
1 vanilla bean

LEMON CAKE Place the chopped apples in your food processor fit with the S-blade and process until smooth. Add the honey, lemon juice, coconut oil, lemon zest, turmeric and salt and process again until well combined. Finally, add the coconut flour and process until completely combined. If your food processor has trouble combining all of the flour, transfer into a large mixing bowl and process the cake in batches. Then mix together all of your batches to make sure the flavors and textures are evenly combined. Divide into four equal portions. Gather two 8" round silicone cake pans and wax paper. Place ¼ of the cake into each silicone pan and press down to flatten. Cover each pressed cake with wax paper, smooth over the cake and flatten any creases. Top each sheet of wax paper with the remaining portions of cake and press to flatten. Set in the freezer for 3 hours to firm.

LEMON COCONUT ICING Place all ingredients in a high-speed blender and blend until very smooth. Place in the refrigerator for 4 hours to firm.

ASSEMBLY Pop one cake layer out of its silicone pan, remove the wax paper and place on a plate. Use a heaping ½ cup of icing to evenly frost the top of the first layer. Repeat for the next two layers. Pop the last cake layer out of its pan and place it on top of the third icing layer. Use the remaining icing to cover the top and sides of the entire cake evenly. Store in the refrigerator or freezer for longer storage, but serve at room temperature. It is lovely with a cup of tea.

* If you do not have access to coconut butter, you can substitute coconut oil, though the consistency will be slightly thinner.

Pure Pleasures

HEAVEN & EARTH CHOCOLATE CAKE

I love anything with white chocolate. As a child I preferred the super sweet and creamy white chocolate to anything dark. Now I love it all and this cake marries the best of both worlds: heavenly white chocolate and deep, earthy, dark chocolate. I made this for the Pure Pleasures cover photo shoot. I went with a cacao butter frosting because I needed something that would hold up in Florida's late July heat. Even at well over 90°F outside, this cake stood strong! As if that was not impressive enough, we immediately dug in at the end of the shoot and wow…pleasure alert!!! Can you even handle it?

Makes one 8" double layer cake

CHOCOLATE CAKE
3 cups peeled and chopped apples
1 cup raw honey
½ cup cold-pressed coconut oil
1⅓ cups raw cacao powder
Seeds of 1 vanilla bean
Pinch of Himalayan salt
2 cups raw coconut flour

WHITE CHOCOLATE ICING
2 cups raw cashews, soaked 2 hours, drained/rinsed
¾ cup raw honey
⅔ cup melted raw cacao butter
6 tablespoons pure water
Seeds of 2 vanilla beans
Generous pinch of Himalayan salt

DARK CHOCOLATE GLOSS
5 tablespoons raw agave nectar
3 tablespoons cold-pressed coconut oil
½ cup raw cacao powder

CHOCOLATE CAKE Place the chopped apples in your food processor fit with the S-blade and process until smooth. Add the honey and coconut oil and process again until well combined. Add the cacao powder, vanilla and salt and continue to process. Finally, add the coconut flour and process until completely combined. If your food processor has trouble combining all of the flour, transfer into a large mixing bowl and process the cake in batches. Then mix together all of your batches to make sure the flavors and textures are evenly combined. Divide the cake into two equal portions and place each half into an 8" round silicone cake pan. If the pan is not silicone, line with wax paper for easy release. Press to flatten and form the cake shape. Set in the freezer for 3 hours to firm.

WHITE CHOCOLATE ICING Combine all ingredients in a high-speed blender and blend until very smooth. Set in the refrigerator for 4 hours to firm.

DARK CHOCOLATE GLOSS Whisk together agave, coconut oil and cacao powder until smooth and shiny.

ASSEMBLY Pop one cake layer out of its silicone pan and place on a plate. Use about one third of the icing to frost just the very top of the cake evenly. Pop the other cake out of its pan and place it on top of the icing layer. Use the remaining icing to cover the top and sides of the entire cake evenly. Drizzle the Dark Chocolate Gloss over the icing in any pretty pattern you like. Store in the refrigerator or freezer for longer storage, but serve at room temperature. Celebrate!!!

Pure Pleasures

VANILLA CAKE
WITH RASPBERRY WHITE CHOCOLATE ICING

A vanilla cake is just classic—a total necessity to have in your repertoire. Here it is paired with a rich raspberry and white chocolate frosting because I wanted something pink like my Birthday cake. Feel free to get creative and mix and match the cake and icing flavors I have shared in this section. I have topped this vanilla cake in countless ways and have loved every one.

Makes one 9" double layer cake

VANILLA CAKE
3 cups peeled and chopped apples
1 tablespoon lemon juice
¾ cup raw honey
½ cup cold-pressed coconut oil
Seeds of 2 vanilla beans
2 teaspoons vanilla extract
Pinch of Himalayan salt
2 cups coconut flour

RASPBERRY WHITE CHOCOLATE ICING
2 cups raspberries
2 cups raw cashews, soaked 2 hours, drained/rinsed
⅔ cup raw cacao butter, melted
½ cup raw honey
¼ teaspoon vanilla extract
Pinch of Himalayan salt
Additional fresh raspberries to garnish

VANILLA CAKE Place the chopped apples in your food processor fit with the S-blade and process until smooth. Immediately add the lemon juice and process to prevent browning. Add the honey, coconut oil, vanilla bean, vanilla extract & salt and process again until well combined. Finally, add the coconut flour and process until completely combined. If your food processor has trouble combining all of the flour, transfer into a large mixing bowl and process the cake in batches. Then mix together all of your batches to make sure the flavors and textures are evenly combined. Divide into two equal portions and place each half into a 9" heart shaped pan, or any desired shape. If the pan is not silicone, line with wax paper for easy release. Press to flatten and form the cake shape. Set in the freezer for 3 hours to firm.

RASPBERRY WHITE CHOCOLATE ICING Place the raspberries in a high-speed blender and blend until smooth. Pour through a sieve to remove the seeds. You will need 1 cup of seedless raspberry purée. Rinse out the blender to remove any remaining seeds. Add the raspberry purée, cashews, cacao butter, honey, vanilla and salt to the clean blender. Blend on high until very smooth. Refrigerate for 4 hours to firm.

Pure Pleasures

ASSEMBLY Pop one cake layer out of its pan and place on a plate. Use about one third of the icing to frost just the very top of the cake evenly. Pop the other cake out of its pan and place it on top of the icing layer. Use the remaining icing to cover the top and sides of the entire cake evenly. Garnish the top with fresh raspberries. Store in the refrigerator or freezer for longer storage, but serve at room temperature. Happy Birthday to me!

RESOURCES

Of course the basis of living food is an abundance of fresh organic fruits and veggies. When I want to have a little extra fun, I get into the specialty ingredients used in some of my more complex recipes. For the best prices and to be sure I am buying truly raw ingredients, I do a lot of shopping through suppliers that I know and trust. Get to know my favorites!

EARTH CIRCLE ORGANICS
12396 Bitney Springs Road, Building #6
Nevada City, CA 95959
1.877.922.FOOD
www.earthcircleorganics.com

Earth Circle Organics offers amazing raw food products to wholesale customers. When I'm talking about really raw cashews and cacao, Earth Circle Organics has got it all. They are very connected with their suppliers and are standing by every product with the utmost integrity.

NATURAL ZING
P.O. Box 749
Mount Airy, MD 21771
1.888.729.9464
www.naturalzing.com

Natural Zing is the largest raw vegan food distributor in the US offering over 1,500 products to consumers, natural food stores, restaurants, and raw food manufacturers. It is owned and operated by its founders. They stock my favorite Coconut Secret products commonly used throughout this book. You'll also find a great selection of lifestyle equipment like blenders, juicers, dehydrators and more. I highly recommend checking out their extensive, high integrity, Natalia approved catalog.

ULTIMATE SUPERFOODS
1.800.728.2066
www.ultimatesuperfoods.com

I turn to Ultimate Superfoods for the best clear, raw agave, superfood powders, super herbs and lots more goodness.

GLASS DHARMA
17900 Ocean Drive #48
Fort Bragg CA 95437
707-964-9350
www.glassdharma.com

Glass Dharma makes the most amazing & beautiful glass straws. Check one out in my Bali Elixir (*page 13*). Once you try a glass straw, you will never touch a disposable one again—and why should you? Think of how many plastic straws we can keep out of landfills if we all make the switch. Oh—and the best part, these have a lifetime guarantee. Glass straws for life, now that's sustainable!

GRATITUDE

My life is full of amazing people and I would love to give my gratitude to all of them for support and inspiration.

Special thanks to my loving family: Adam, for completely being by my side every step of the way in life and with this book. To Mom, for more inspiration than I know what to do with and for always nourishing me. To Dad, for always telling me how proud he is and always making sure I'm really okay. To Justin, for having a solid answer to any question I come up with, be it in the kitchen or in life...and for feeding me. To Robin, for joining up with the KW shenanigans without missing a beat. To Ian, for keeping me on my toes when it comes to inspiring young minds. To my Babushka, for always reminding me to have something sweet after dinner. To Uncle John & Janina, for always making me laugh around the table.

To the Mills family for their unconditional love and support, Judi, David, Brian, Amy, Grandma, Barbara, Donald & Holly.

To my beautiful friends: Addie, my oldest friend, for the wonderful memories and for the amazing Jungle Ball inspiration. To Cylleria, for really being there for me, always. To Cynthia, for the book know-how. To Danielle, for sharing many experimental meals together as young ones. To Ishvara, for waking me up to find my true purpose. To Jaszy, as a friend and through Modern Hippie Mag, for amazing promotion. To Jerah, for always being up to chat business and for the hot photos. To Kate, for strongly supporting my dreams even when it meant me skipping town. To Tyler, for being my first friend in Florida and for sharing in some of the best salad parties ever. To Wendy, for unparalleled love and support, for selflessly gifting me hours of her time to be in my kitchen and for loaning me some fabulous plates for photography. Also to her boys, Trevor and Tegan, for giving me the kid seal of approval for my food.

To Ishvara, Hugo, Boni, Chava and all of the mi Pueblo family—thank you for co-creating a beautiful live food menu with me and for helping to share my dreams on a much larger scale. To all that I worked with at Veggie Magic—thank you for an amazing year. To Chris and Eva Worden and all of the Worden Farms staff (like Tobie!) for the most beautiful organic veggies I could ever dream of and for the super friendly service. To Jessica's Organic Farm, my weekly stop for gorgeous organic produce grown right in Sarasota. To Peter Burkard, for always having something exotic at his farm stand. To King Farms for the best peaches and blueberries that I have ever tasted. Also to The Granary and Whole Foods Market Sarasota for sustaining me during the hot Florida Summers. To Earth Circle Organics, Natural Zing, Ultimate Superfoods, Glass Dharma and Coconut Secret for your top quality, high integrity products.

To Modern Hippie Mag, the Green Girls and G Living, thank you for helping me share my passion with the world.

To those who have been supporting me and Glowing Temple since the very beginnings, giving me the confidence to keep going with the flow…and to YOU for supporting my vision by purchasing this book, I am grateful.

Made in the USA
Charleston, SC
30 April 2011